Manhattan Review

Test Prep & Admissions Consulting

Turbocharge Your GMAT:
Combinatorics & Probability Guide

5th Edition (December 18th, 2012)

☐ *Intuitive and graphical explanations of concepts*

☐ *130 GMAT-like practice questions*

  · *Permutation & Combination – 65 Questions*
  · *Probability – 65 Questions*
  · *Ample questions with Alternate Approaches*

☐ *Detailed explanation of solutions*

☐ *Mapped according to the scope of the GMAT*

www.manhattanreview.com

Copyright and Terms of Use

10-Digit International Standard Book Number: (ISBN: 1629260304)
13-Digit International Standard Book Number: (ISBN: 978-1-62926-030-3)

Last updated on December 18, 2012.

Manhattan Review, 275 Madison Avenue, Suite 424, New York, NY 10016.
Phone: +1 (212) 316-2000. E-Mail: info@manhattanreview.com. Web: www.manhattanreview.com

About the Turbocharge your GMAT Series

The Turbocharge Your GMAT series is designed to be clear and comprehensive. It is the set of tools you need to build the success you seek. Manhattan Review has created these guides to lead you through the complexities of the examination and achieve your best possible result. As so many students before you have discovered, our books break down the different test sections in a careful, clear manner and zero in on exactly what you need to know to raise your score. The complete series is designed to be your best GMAT test prep companion as you navigate the road to a successful outcome.

- ☐ **GMAT Math Study Guide** (ISBN: 978-1-62926-013-6)
- ☐ **GMAT Math Study Companion** (ISBN: 978-1-62926-014-3)
- ☐ **GMAT Verbal Study Guide** (ISBN: 978-1-62926-015-0)
- ☐ **GMAT Verbal Study Companion** (ISBN: 978-1-62926-016-7)
- ☐ **GMAT Math Essentials** (ISBN: 978-1-62926-017-4)
- ☐ **GMAT Number Properties** (ISBN: 978-1-62926-018-1)
- ☐ **GMAT Arithmetic** (ISBN: 978-1-62926-019-8)
- ☐ **GMAT Algebra** (ISBN: 978-1-62926-020-4)
- ☐ **GMAT Geometry** (ISBN: 978-1-62926-021-1)
- ☐ **GMAT Word Problems** (ISBN: 978-1-62926-028-0)
- ☐ **GMAT Sets & Statistics** (ISBN: 978-1-62926-029-7)
- ■ **GMAT Combinatorics & Probability** (ISBN: 978-1-62926-030-3)
- ☐ **GMAT Sentence Correction Guide** (ISBN: 978-1-62926-022-8)
- ☐ **GMAT Critical Reasoning Guide** (ISBN: 978-1-62926-023-5)
- ☐ **GMAT Reading Comprehension Guide** (ISBN: 978-1-62926-024-2)
- ☐ **GMAT Integrated Reasoning Guide** (ISBN: 978-1-62926-025-9)
- ☐ **GMAT Analytical Writing Guide** (ISBN: 978-1-62926-026-6)
- ☐ **GMAT Vocabulary Builder** (ISBN: 978-1-62926-027-3)

About the Company

Manhattan Review's origin can be traced directly to an Ivy-League MBA classroom in 1999. While lecturing on advanced quantitative subjects to MBAs at Columbia Business School in New York City, Professor Dr. Joern Meissner was asked by his students to assist their friends, who were frustrated with conventional GMAT preparation options. He started to create original lectures that focused on presenting GMAT content in a coherent and concise manner rather than as a download of voluminous basic knowledge interspersed with so-called "tricks." The new approach immediately proved highly popular with GMAT students, inspiring the birth of Manhattan Review. Over the past 15+ years, Manhattan Review has grown into a multi-national firm, focusing on GMAT, GRE, LSAT, SAT, and TOEFL test prep and tutoring, along with business school, graduate school, and college admissions consulting; application advisory, and essay editing services.

About the Founder

Professor Joern Meissner, the founder and chairman of Manhattan Review, has over twenty-five years of teaching experience in undergraduate and graduate programs at prestigious business schools in the USA, UK, and Germany. He created the original lectures, which are constantly updated by the Manhattan Review Team to reflect the evolving nature of GMAT, GRE, LSAT, SAT, and TOEFL test prep and private tutoring. Professor Meissner received his Ph.D. in Management Science from the Graduate School of Business at Columbia University (Columbia Business School) in New York City and is a recognized authority in the area of Supply Chain Management (SCM), Dynamic Pricing, and Revenue Management. Currently, he holds the position of Full Professor of Supply Chain Management and Pricing Strategy at Kuehne Logistics University in Hamburg, Germany. Professor Meissner is a passionate and enthusiastic teacher. He believes that grasping an idea is only half of the fun; conveying it to others makes it whole. At his previous position at Lancaster University Management School, he taught the MBA Core course in Operations Management and originated three new MBA Electives: Advanced Decision Models, Supply Chain Management, and Revenue Management. He has also lectured at the University of Hamburg, the Leipzig Graduate School of Management (HHL), and the University of Mannheim. Professor Meissner offers a variety of Executive Education courses aimed at business professionals, managers, leaders, and executives who strive for professional and personal growth. He frequently advises companies ranging from Fortune 500 companies to emerging start-ups on various issues related to his research expertise. Please visit his academic homepage www.meiss.com for further information.

Manhattan Review Advantages

▶ **Time Efficiency and Cost Effectiveness**

- The most limiting factor in test preparation for most people is time.
- It takes significantly more teaching experience and techniques to prepare a student in less time.
- Our preparation is tailored for busy professionals. We will teach you what you need to know in the least amount of time.

▶ **High-quality and dedicated instructors who are committed to helping every student reach her/his goals**

▶ **Manhattan Review's team members have combined wisdom of**

- Academic achievements
- MBA teaching experience at prestigious business schools in the US and UK
- Career success

**Visit us at www.ManhattanReview.com and
find out which courses are available close to *you*!**

International Phone Numbers & Official Manhattan Review Websites

Manhattan Headquarters	+1-212-316-2000	www.manhattanreview.com
USA & Canada	+1-800-246-4600	www.manhattanreview.com
Australia	+61-3-9001-6618	www.manhattanreview.com
Austria	+43-720-115-549	www.review.at
Belgium	+32-2-808-5163	www.manhattanreview.be
China	+86-20-2910-1913	www.manhattanreview.cn
Czech Republic	+1-212-316-2000	www.review.cz
France	+33-1-8488-4204	www.review.fr
Germany	+49-89-3803-8856	www.review.de
Greece	+1-212-316-2000	www.review.com.gr
Hong Kong	+852-5808-2704	www.review.hk
Hungary	+1-212-316-2000	www.review.co.hu
India	+1-212-316-2000	www.review.in
Indonesia	+1-212-316-2000	www.manhattanreview.com
Ireland	+1-212-316-2000	www.gmat.ie
Italy	+39-06-9338-7617	www.manhattanreview.it
Japan	+81-3-4589-5125	www.manhattanreview.jp
Malaysia	+1-212-316-2000	www.manhattanreview.com
Netherlands	+31-20-808-4399	www.manhattanreview.nl
Philippines	+1-212-316-2000	www.review.ph
Poland	+1-212-316-2000	www.review.pl
Portugal	+1-212-316-2000	www.review.pt
Russia	+1-212-316-2000	www.manhattanreview.ru
Singapore	+65-3158-2571	www.gmat.sg
South Africa	+1-212-316-2000	www.manhattanreview.co.za
South Korea	+1-212-316-2000	www.manhattanreview.kr
Sweden	+1-212-316-2000	www.gmat.se
Spain	+34-911-876-504	www.review.es
Switzerland	+41-435-080-991	www.review.ch
Taiwan	+1-212-316-2000	www.gmat.tw
Thailand	+66-6-0003-5529	www.manhattanreview.com
United Arab Emirates	+1-212-316-2000	www.manhattanreview.ae
United Kingdom	+44-20-7060-9800	www.manhattanreview.co.uk
Rest of the World	+1-212-316-2000	www.manhattanreview.com

Contents

Chapter 1

Welcome

Dear Students,

Here at Manhattan Review, we constantly strive to provide you the best educational content for standardized test preparation. We make a tremendous effort to keep making things better and better for you. This is especially important with respect to an examination such as the GMAT. A typical GMAT aspirant is confused with so many test-prep options available. Your challenge is to choose a book or a tutor that prepares you for attaining your goal. We cannot say that we are one of the best, it is you who has to be the judge.

There are umpteen numbers of books on Quantitative Ability for GMAT preparation. What is so different about this book? The answer lies in its approach to deal with the questions. The book is meant to develop your fundamentals on one of the most talked about topic on GMAT-Quants–Permutation & Combination and Probability. The concepts are explained with the help of text-cum-graphic aid. It is a treat to read the book along with relevant graphics. Pictures speak louder than words!

You will find a lot of variety in the problems discussed. Alternate approaches to few tricky questions are worth appreciating. We have tried to rope in the options, a typical GMAT test-maker prepares to trap you and duly explained how to get rid of those.

Apart from books on 'Number Properties', 'Word Problem', 'Algebra', 'Arithmetic', 'Geometry', 'Sets and Statistics', and 'Data Sufficiency', which are solely dedicated on GMAT-Quantitative Ability, the book on 'GMAT Math Essentials' is solely dedicated to develop your math fundamentals.

The Manhattan Review's 'GMAT-Combinatorics and Probability' book is holistic and comprehensive in all respects. Should you have any queries, please feel free to write to me at info@manhattanreview.com.

Happy Learning!

Professor Dr. Joern Meissner
& The Manhattan Review Team

Chapter 2

Combinatorics

Combinatorics can be called the **science of counting**. This is the branch of mathematics in which we study the selection and/or the arrangement of the elements of finite sets, having certain characteristics.

We seek to find out the answers to the questions like:

"In how many ways can a team of 4 members be selected from 10 people?"

or

"In how many possible ways can different photographs be taken of a group of people standing in a line, considering that a different order results in a new photograph?"

or

"How many ten-digit phone numbers starting with "98" are possible?"

There are two parts to Combinatorics, namely, **Permutation**, and **Combination**. These can also be called **Counting Methods**.

Combinatorics topic has attracted a fair amount of attention on the GMAT recently. It is also a vital topic from the perspective of probability, which is frequently tested on the GMAT.

2.1 Permutation

 The notion of permutation implies the act of permuting or arranging few objects. Permutation of a set of objects is an act of arranging them in a particular order. For example, there are six possible permutations (arrangements) of the set (A, B, C), namely (A, B, C), (A, C, B), (B, A, C), (B, C, A), (C, A, B), and (C, B, A).

2.2 Combination

 The notion of combination is a way of selecting one or several objects out of a set, where the order or the arrangement of objects does not matter. In the above example, selection of all the three objects from the set (A, B, C), namely (A, B, C) is possible in only one way. Arranging the elements as (A, C, B), (B, A, C), (B, C, A), (C, A, B), and (C, B, A) does not make any difference as the same objects are there in each set.

However, if we select only two objects from the set (A, B, C), then there are three possible selections, namely (A, B), (A, C), and (B, C). Sets (B, A), (C, A), and (C, B) do not make a different selection as the order is not important.

Similarly, if we select only one object from the set, then there are three possible selections, namely (A), (B), and (C).

2.3   What's the difference?

We use the word "combination" casually in daily lives, without bothering whether the order of objects is important. Let's see examples.

If I say that the vehicle registration number of my car is formed out of four digits: 0, 2, 5, and 6, can you guess what could be the number? Well, it's not possible to guess correctly as there are many possible numbers out of 0, 2, 5, and 6. If we arrange 0, 2, 5, and 6, there are, for example, 2056, 5602, 6205, and many more numbers. Just for your curiosity, there are as many as 24 possible numbers out of these 4 digits. This calls for **permutation.**

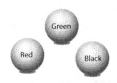

If I say to you that I have three colored balls—red, green, and black.   Had it made any difference if I had rather said that I have three colored balls—green, red, and black?— No; as the order in not important.   This calls for **combination.**

In other words—*A Permutation is an ordered Combination.*

Combinatorics	Selection is important	Order/Arrangement is important
• Permutation	Yes	Yes
• Combination	Yes	No

2.4 Permutation

Let us develop a formulaic approach to solve lengthy questions.

Question: In how many ways can Alex, Betty, and Chris get photographed?

> The foremost decision in the Permutation & Combination based question is to ask which of the two concepts needs to be applied in the question? The answer is: ask yourself whether the arrangement of the objects will render a unique way or a presentation. If the answer is yes, apply permutation, else combination.
>
> In the above question, the arrangement is important as the photograph of Betty, Alex, and Chris (standing in that order) will be different from the photograph of Alex, Betty, and Chris (standing in that order); so, we will apply permutation.

Develop a formula

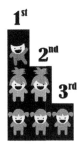 There are a total of three places to be occupied by Alex, Betty, and Chris. They can stand in any order to get photographed. The first place can be occupied in three ways: any one of Alex, Betty, and Chris will stand on the first place; similarly, the second place can be occupied in only two ways as one of Alex, Betty, and Chris has already occupied the first place; and the last place can be occupied in only one way as two of Alex, Betty, and Chris have already occupied the first, and the second place.

So, the **total number of ways** = 3 × 2 × 1 = **6 ways.**

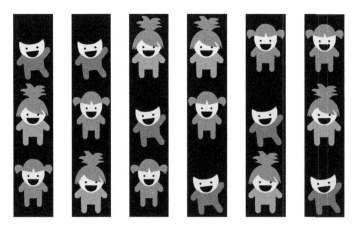

What if there are n number of friends who want to get photographed?

In a similar way, the first place can be occupied in n number of ways: any one of n friends will stand here; similarly, the second place can be occupied in $(n-1)$ ways as one of n friends has already occupied the first place; similarly, the third place can be occupied in $(n-2)$ ways as two of n friends have already occupied the first and the second place; and the last place can be occupied in only one way.

So, **the total number of ways** $= n \times (n-1) \times (n-2) \times (n-3) \times (n-4) \times \ldots\ldots\ldots 1 = n!$.

$n!$ is called factorial n. Its value equals to the product of all the integers from '1' to 'n'.

Selecting few objects from all the objects

Say, if any **two** of Alex, Betty, and Chris are to be photographed, then in how many ways can they be photographed?

Now, there are only two places to be occupied by any two of Alex, Betty, and Chris. The first place can be occupied by 3 ways, and the second place can be occupied by 2 ways.

So, the **total number of ways** $= 3 \times 2 = 6$ **ways.**
What if there are r friends out of n friends to get photographed?

On a similar way, the first place can be occupied in n ways; the second place can be occupied in $(n-1)$ ways; the third place can be occupied in $(n-2)$ ways; and similarly, the rth place can be occupied in $(n-r+1)$ or $[n-(r-1)]$ ways.

So, the **total number of ways** $= n \times (n-1) \times (n-2) \times (n-3) \times \ldots\ldots\ldots [n-(r-1)]$

In mathematical notations, it is written as P_r^n or $P(n,r)$.

So, P_r^n or $P(n,r) = n \times (n-1) \times (n-2) \times (n-3) \times \ldots\ldots\ldots[n-(r-1)]$;

If $r = n$, then P_n^n or $P(n,n) = n \times (n-1) \times (n-2) \times (n-3) \times \ldots\ldots\ldots 1 = n!$.

If we need to find the permutations of r distinct objects out of n distinct objects, we apply:

$$P_r^n = \frac{n!}{(n-r)!} \text{ ; and } P_n^n = n!$$

Some most common values of factorials:

- $5! = 5 \times 4 \times 3 \times 2 \times 1 = 120$
- $4! = 4 \times 3 \times 2 \times 1 = 24$
- $3! = 3 \times 2 \times 1 = 6$
- $2! = 2 \times 1 = 2$

- **1! = 1**
- **0! = 1** (you may by surprised that the value of 0! is '1', but it is so.)

Question: In how many ways can 3 out of 4 friends be photographed?

    Solution: The number of ways = 4.3.2 = 24 ways.

    Formula approach: $n = 4$, and $r = 3$; so, $P_3^4 = \dfrac{4!}{(4-3)!} = \dfrac{4!}{1!} = 4.3.2.1 = 24$ ways.

Question: In how many ways can all 4 friends be photographed?

    Solution: The number of ways = 4! = 4.3.2.1 = 24 ways.

    Formula approach: $n = 4$, and $r = 4$; so, $P_4^4 = \dfrac{4!}{(4-4)!} = \dfrac{4!}{0!} = \dfrac{4.3.2.1}{1} = 24$ ways.

2.4.1   Permutation with repetition of objects

In the examples above, we tried to find out the number ways 3 friends can be photographed. In the example, you must have noticed that each successive place has one less way to get filled. It is because if, say, Betty occupied the first place, she cannot occupy the second or the third place.

Let us see the following example.

Question: How many 3-digit combination codes with digits 1, 2, and 3 are possible for a lock?

    If your answer is 3! = 6 combinations, you assumed that NO digit can be repeated. Say, if the digit '2' occupied the first place, it cannot reappear in the second and the third place.

    However, in a real life, there can be a combination code such as '333', which means that the digits can be repeated.

    So, if the digits can be repeated, the possible number of combinations $= 3 \times 3 \times 3 = 27$.

    If there are n digits, and n to be filled, the **total number of ways = n^n**, if repetition is allowed.

Let us see following example.

Question: How many 3-digit passwords are possible with the digits 0, 1, 2 .... 9? Repetition is allowed.

Since each place can be filled in 10 ways (any digit among 0 to 9 may be used), the total number of possible passwords = $10 \times 10 \times 10 = 10^3 = 1000$.

Similarly, for a question: how many r-digit passwords are possible with n digits, if repetition of digits is allowed?

The answer would be $n \times n \times n \times ....r$ times = n^r passwords.

Number of arrangements out of selecting r objects from n objects = n^r; Repetition is allowed.

Remember that it is important to know beforehand whether repetition is allowed. If it is NOT allowed, then for the above example, the answer would be $P_r^n = \dfrac{n!}{(n-r)!}$.

2.4.2 Circular permutation

We have already seen the question: In how many ways can Alex, Betty, and Chris get seated?

The answer to the question is 3! = 6 ways. It is implied that all three will stand in a row. What if the question were:

In how many distinct ways can Alex, Betty, and Chris get seated around a <u>round table</u>?

Well, the answer would be (3 − 1)! = 2! = only 2 ways! This is because, unlike the arrangement in a line, merely by moving from one place to the other does not make a distinct seating arrangement with a round table.

If there are n objects to be arranged in a **circle**, in which all the positions are identical, we need to assign one of the objects to a seat to mark it as the starting point (since in a circle, there is no distinct starting point). Thus, there are $(n-1)$ objects left to be arranged. So, these n objects can be arranged in $(n-1)!$ ways.

Let us see how.

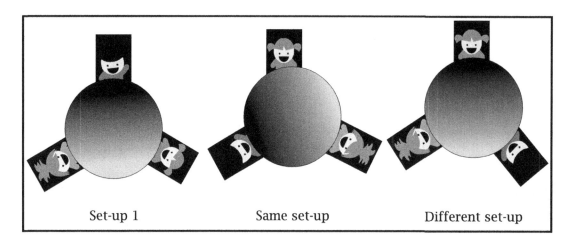

| Set-up 1 | Same set-up | Different set-up |

So, the number of distinct ways n objects can be arranged in a straight line = $n!$;

but,

The number of distinct ways n objects can be arranged around a circle = $(n - 1)!$

2.5 Combination

Let us develop a formulaic approach to solve lengthy questions.

Question: In how many ways can two balls out of three balls (a red, a green, and a black) be selected?

As stated earlier that the foremost decision in the Permutation & Combination based questions is to ask which of the two concepts needs to be applied? Ask yourself whether the arrangement of two balls selected will render a unique selection. If the answer is yes, apply permutation, else combination.

In the above question, the arrangement is not important as, if the two selected balls are, say, red and green, it is does not matter whether they are **red and green** or **green and red**; so, we will apply combination.

Develop the formula

Two balls selected can either be **red and green, red and black** or **green and black**, so there are total three ways (RG/RB/GB).

What if the order was given importance, though conceptually wrong in this case, the answer would have been $P_2^3 = 3.2 = 6$ ways (wrong answer).

So, the correct answer can be written as $\dfrac{P_2^3}{2!} = \dfrac{6}{2} = 3$ ways.

So, if r different objects are to be selected out of n different objects, then the total number of ways would be $C_r^n = \dfrac{P_r^n}{r!} = \dfrac{n!}{r!(n-r)!}$

$$\boxed{C_r^n = \dfrac{n!}{r!(n-r)!}}$$

$$\boxed{C_r^n = \dfrac{n.(n-1).(n-2).(n-3).....[n-(r-1)]}{[r.(r-1).(r-2).....1]}}$$

Question: In how many ways can 4 out of 6 balls be drawn from an urn?

Total number of ways = $C_4^6 = \dfrac{6!}{4!(6-4)!} = \dfrac{6!}{4!(2)!} = \dfrac{6.5.4.3.2.1}{(2.1)(4.3.2.1)} = 15$ ways.

Alternate approach 1:

Above approach to calculate the value of C_4^6 is lengthy. It could have been calculated using the following approach. See the next question.

Question: In how many ways can 5 out of 7 balls be drawn from an urn?

Total number of ways = $C_5^7 = \dfrac{7.6.\cancel{5}.\cancel{4}.\cancel{3}}{\cancel{5}.\cancel{4}.\cancel{3}.2.1} = 21$ ways.

Alternate approach 2:

The calculation of C_5^7 can further be simplified; you would have observed that 5, 4, and 3 are getting cancelled from the numerator and the denominator.

However, C_5^7 can be rewritten as $C_{(7-2)}^7$ and is equal to $C_2^7 = \dfrac{7.6}{2.1} = 21$ ways. So,

$$\boxed{C_r^n = C_{(n-r)}^n}$$

But, remember that

$$\boxed{P_r^n \neq P_{(n-r)}^n}$$

Note: Apply Alternate approach 2, if $r > (n - r)$

Question: In how many ways can 2 out of 7 balls be drawn from an urn?

Total number of ways = $C_2^7 = \dfrac{7.6}{2.1} = 21$ ways; however, in this case, we must not transform C_2^7 to $C_{(7-5)}^7$, as this will rather lengthen the calculation, however the answer would be the same.

2.6 Concepts Revisited

Question	Permutation or Combination	Should we apply $C_r^n = C_{(n-r)}^n$?	Solution
In how many ways can 4 out of 6 friends be seated in a row?	**Permutation;** Order is important	Not applicable for permutation	# of ways = 6.5.4.3 = 360 ways
In how many ways can 12 out of 14 players be selected for a team?	**Combination;** Order is not important; only selection the matters.	Yes; as $r > n - r$ $r = 12 \ \& \ n = 14$	# of ways = $C_{12}^{14} = C_2^{14} =$ 14.13/1.2 = 91 ways
In how many ways can 5 different colored balls be arranged in a row to show distinguishable patterns?	**Permutation;** Order is important. Remember that not every question on balls is a combination question.	Not applicable for permutation	# of ways = 5! = 5.4.3.2.1 = 120 ways
In how many ways can 5 different colored balls be arranged around a circle to show distinguishable patterns?	**Circular Permutation;** Order is important	Not applicable for permutation	# of ways = $(5 - 1)! = 4! =$ 4.3.2.1 = 24 ways
In how many ways can 2 out of 6 players be selected for a team?	**Combination;** Order is not important; only the selection matters.	No; $r < n - r$ $r = 2 \ \& \ n = 6$	# of ways = $C_2^6 = 6.5/1.2 =$ 15 ways
In how many ways can all players out of 6 players be selected for a team?	**Combination;** Order is not important; only the selection matters.	Though yes, it is not needed.	For a combination question, if $r = n$ or $r = 0$, # of ways is ALWAYS equal to 1.

2.7   Permutation of multiple indistinguishable objects

Question: How many meaningful or meaningless words can be formed out of the word 'book'?

The answer '4! = 24 words' is a wrong answer as two O's were counted as different letters, but they are the same.

If there are multiple indistinguishable objects, we must exclude the number of ways formed because of them as they are basically the same.

Total number of words = $\dfrac{4!}{2!}$ = 12 words; the 2! in the denominator is for two O's. The 12 words would be **book, boko, bkoo, kboo, kobo, koob, oobk, ookb, okob, obok, obko, & okbo.**

Develop a formula

If there are total n balls, and among these, there are p number of identical green, q number of identical red, and r number of identical black balls, in how many ways can these balls be arranged in a row to have unique patterns?

$$\text{Total number of ways} = \frac{n!}{p!.q!.r!}$$

Question: How many words with or without meaning can be formed out of the word 'Mississippi'?

There are total 11 letters, so n = 11; there are four I's, so p = 4; four S's, so q = 4; two P's, so r = 2.

So, total number of words = $\dfrac{11!}{4!.4!.2!}$ = $\dfrac{11!}{2(4!)^2}$ words

2.8   Restricted Permutation

Question: How many 4-digit even numbers can be formed out of digits 0-10? Repetition is allowed.

This is a question on restricted permutation. We not only have to find the count of 4-digit numbers, but also assure that the numbers are even. It implies that the unit digits must be either 0, 2, 4, 6, or 8—only 5 ways; the unit place can be filled in five ways.

Also the digit at the thousandth place cannot be '0', as allowing '0' at the thousandth place will render 3-digit numbers. It implies that the thousandth place digit must be any digit among (1-9): 9 possibilities.

So, total # of 4-digit numbers

= [# of ways to fill thousandth place] $\times$ [# of ways to fill hundredth place] $\times$ [# of ways to fill tenth place] $\times$ [# of ways to fill unit place]

= $9 \times 10 \times 10 \times 5 = 4500$ numbers.

2.9   Restricted Combination

Question: In how many ways can 3 out of 11 players of a team be selected, if the captain must be included in the selection?

Since the captain must be included, the question becomes: In how many ways can 2 out of 10 players of a team be selected?, as one selection (the captain) is already done.

# of ways = $C_2^{10} = 10.9/1.2 = 45$ ways.

If the question is changed to: In how many ways can 3 out of 11 players of a team be selected, provided the captain should NOT be included in the selection?

Since the captain is not to be included, the question becomes: In how many ways can 3 out of 10 players of a team be selected?, as one player (the captain) is out of the selection process.

# of ways = $C_3^{10} = 10.9.8/1.2.3 = 120$ ways.

Let us see another question with two different set of objects.

Question: In how many ways can a man choose 2 trousers and 3 shirts out of 3 trousers and 4 shirts?

Let's choose trousers first. # of ways to choose trousers = $C_2^3 = C_1^3 = 3$ ways; $[C_r^n = C_{(n-r)}^n]$

Let's choose shirts now. # of ways to choose shirts = $C_3^4 = C_1^4 = 4$ ways;

Total number of ways of choosing 2 trousers and 3 shirts = $3 \times 4 = 12$ ways.

2.10   Rule of Sum

If there are 4 boys and 3 girls, in how many ways can a team of 2 be formed such that there are either both the boys or both the girls in the team?

# of ways 2 boys can be selected = $C_2^4 = 4.3/1.2 = 6$ ways;

# of ways 2 girls can be selected = $C_2^3 = C_1^3 = 3$ ways;

Since either of the ways can occur, so the total number of ways either two boys or two girls can be selected = 6 + 3 = 9 ways.

The key word is EITHER.

If an event can be done in two or more ways, the numbers of ways are added. This is called **'Rule of Sum'**.

2.11   Rule of Product

If there are 4 boys and 3 girls, in how many ways can a team of 4 be formed such that there must be 2 boys and 2 girls in the team?

# of ways 2 boys can be selected = $C_2^4 = 4.3/1.2 = 6$ ways;

# of ways 2 girls can be selected = $C_2^3 = C_1^3 = 3$ ways;

Since selecting 4 members is composed of selecting 2 boys and 2 girls, so the total number of ways 4 members would be selected = 6 × 3 = 18 ways.

The key word is AND.

If an event is composed of two or more sub-events, total number of ways of doing the event equals to the product of the total number of ways of doing each of the sub-event. This is called **'Rule of Product'**.

Key word	Total # of ways
• Either or	Add the number of ways (+)
• And	Multiply the number of ways (×)

Chapter 3

Practice Questions

3.1 Problem Solving

1. 4-digit numbers are formed using the digits 3, 4, 8, and 9. Repetition of digits is allowed. How many of these numbers would be even?

    (A) 56

    (B) 85

    (C) 110

    (D) 128

    (E) 170

    Solve yourself:

2. How many different license numbers can be allotted using 3 letters and 3 digits? All the letters and all the digits must appear together. Repetition of the letters and the digits is allowed.

    (A) $C_3^{26}.C_3^{10}$

    (B) $2.C_3^{26}.C_3^{10}$

    (C) $26^3.10^2$

    (D) $2.26^3.10^3$

    (E) $26^3.10^3$

    Solve yourself:

3. How many 5-digit numbers can be formed containing exactly one '3'? Other digits can be repeated.

    (A) $4.C_4^9$

    (B) $5.C_4^9$

    (C) $4.8.9^4$

    (D) $4.9^4 + 9^3$

    (E) $9^4 + 4.8.9^3$

Solve yourself:

4. There are 8 different locks, with exactly one key for each lock. All the keys have been mixed up. What is maximum number of trials needed to determine which key belongs to which lock?

(A) 14

(B) 28

(C) 56

(D) 64

(E) 128

Solve yourself:

5. Captain of a team can select only n players out of $(2n + 1)$ players. If the total number of ways, he can select the players is 126, what is the value of n?

(A) 2

(B) 3

(C) 4

(D) 5

(E) 6

Solve yourself:

6. In a polygon of 8 equal sides, how many different triangles can be drawn using the vertices of the polygon as the vertices of the triangles?

(A) 24
(B) 28
(C) 56
(D) 64
(E) 72

Solve yourself:

7. A puzzle can be solved by choosing 1 cube from the puzzle box1 containing 10 cubes, and 2 cubes from the puzzle box2 containing 5 cubes. In how many ways can the puzzle be solved?

(A) 50
(B) 64
(C) 100
(D) 128
(E) 200

Solve yourself:

8. How many numbers less than 1000 can be formed out of digits 3, 4, 5, and 6?

(A) 16
(B) 64
(C) 84
(D) 128
(E) 340

Solve yourself:

9. How many 2-member teams can be formed from 5 individuals provided 2 specific individuals together must not be in the team?

   (A) 3

   (B) 6

   (C) 8

   (D) 9

   (E) 10

   Solve yourself:

10. In how many ways can 2 boys and 2 girls be chosen from a class comprising 10 boys and 12 girls?

   (A) 111

   (B) 240

   (C) 480

   (D) 2970

   (E) 11880

   Solve yourself:

11. How many 5-letter words can be formed if the first letter and the last letter are vowels?

   (A) $2.5^2.26^3$

   (B) $5^2.26^3$

   (C) $2.5^2.21^3$

   (D) $5^2.21^3$

   (E) $5^3.21^2$

Solve yourself:

12. How many 5-letter codes can be formed out of letters *c, k, m, t, & u* such that no code starts with '*muc* _ _'? Repetition of letters is allowed.

   (A) $5^5 - 3^5$
   (B) $5^5 + 2^5$
   (C) $5^5 - 2^5$
   (D) $5^5 - 5^2$
   (E) $5^5 + 5^2$

   Solve yourself:

13. A criminal speaks either the truth or the lie for each of three questions. For us to know the fact, he must speak the truth for each question. In how many ways can be hide the truth?

   (A) 2
   (B) 3
   (C) 7
   (D) 8
   (E) 26

   Solve yourself:

14. There are 5 differently colored cubes. In how many ways can a child arrange them in a row taking only 3 cubes at a time such that the arrangements make unique patterns?

(A) 6

(B) 10

(C) 15

(D) 60

(E) 120

Solve yourself:

15. How many distinct words with or without meaning can be formed using all the letters of the word "APPEALING"?

(A) $\dfrac{9!}{2! \cdot 2!}$

(B) $\dfrac{9!}{2}$

(C) $7!$

(D) $9!$

(E) $9! \cdot 2! \cdot 2!$

Solve yourself:

16. In the question given above, how many words will have L and G together (in any order)?

(A) $\dfrac{8!}{2! \cdot 2!}$

(B) $\dfrac{8!}{2!}$

(C) $8!$

(D) $8! \cdot 2!$

(E) $\dfrac{9!}{2! \cdot 2!}$

Solve yourself:

17. In the question given above, how many words are possible when all the vowels occur together?

    (A) 72
    (B) 144
    (C) 1728
    (D) 3456
    (E) 4320

    Solve yourself:

18. A school wishes to select 11 students for an annual parade out of 15 students with similar height. In how many ways can the school make a selection, if the order of selection does not matter?

    (A) 165
    (B) 1365
    (C) 11!
    (D) 1365.(11!)
    (E) $(11!)^2$

    Solve yourself:

19. UN peacekeeping force wants to form a delegation of 5 generals. It wants to choose 2 out of 5 generals from UK and 3 out of 6 generals from France. In how many ways can the selection be done?

    (A)   100

    (B)   200

    (C)   462

    (D)   100.(5!)

    (E)   11!

    Solve yourself:

20.   A casting director wishes to cast 5 actors out of 13 shortlisted TV actors for his movies. Out of 13 actors, 5 actors act in soaps, and 8 actors act in reality TV shows. In how many ways can the director select the actors such that there are 2 actors from soaps and 3 actors from reality TV shows?

    (A)   66

    (B)   110

    (C)   356

    (D)   560

    (E)   6720

    Solve yourself:

21.   A soccer selection panel has to select 15 probable players out of 17 players such that the captain is always selected and an injured player is not selected. In how many ways can the selection be done?

    (A)   15

    (B)   120

    (C)   136

    (D)   560

    (E)   680

Solve yourself:

22. How many 3-element subsets of a set {A, B, C, D, E} are possible such that they do not contain the subset of elements A, C, & D?

    (A) 5
    (B) 6
    (C) 9
    (D) 50
    (E) 54

    Solve yourself:

23. There are 10 male and 8 female dancers in a club. If the club is to form two groups, each having 1 male and 1 female dancer, in how many ways it can be done?

    (A) 143
    (B) 160
    (C) 1260
    (D) 2520
    (E) 5040

    Solve yourself:

24. A cricket team of 11 players is to be chosen from 8 batsmen, 6 bowlers and 2 wicket-keepers. In how many ways, can the team be chosen if there must be at least 4 batsmen, at least 4 bowlers and exactly 1 wicket-keeper?

(A) 140

(B) 672

(C) 840

(D) 1652

(E) 6504

Solve yourself:

25. In how many ways can a person choose between four types of salads and six types of toppings for a pizza?

(A) 10

(B) 24

(C) 48

(D) 96

(E) 1024

Solve yourself:

26. How many seven-digit telephone numbers starting with 2431 are possible, so that the string of the last three digits neither starts nor ends with '0'?

(A) 648

(B) 729

(C) 810

(D) 900

(E) 1000

Solve yourself:

27. In how many ways can three men and two women be selected from four men and three women?

   (A) 5
   (B) 6
   (C) 12
   (D) 15
   (E) 20

   Solve yourself:

28. How many three-digit numbers without repetition of digits can be formed using the digits 0, 2, 3, 5 so that they are even?

   (A) 6
   (B) 10
   (C) 15
   (D) 20
   (E) 40

   Solve yourself:

29. John has four friends. In how many ways can he invite one or more of his friends to a party?

   (A) 8
   (B) 15
   (C) 16
   (D) 31
   (E) 63

Solve yourself:

30. What is the number of ways in which the letters of the word RANDOM can be arranged in a circle so that the letters A, N, D come together in that order to form 'AND'?

    (A) 2

    (B) 3

    (C) 6

    (D) 8

    (E) 9

    Solve yourself:

31. What is the number of ways in which the letters of INDIANA be arranged?

    (A) 630

    (B) 700

    (C) 729

    (D) 800

    (E) 810

    Solve yourself:

32. A 5-member team has to be formed for a debate competition and the speaker for the team has to be decided from among its members. If there are eight members from whom the team has to be picked, in how many ways it can be formed and the speaker is decided?

(A) 100

(B) 200

(C) 280

(D) 300

(E) 360

Solve yourself:

33. In how many ways can four boys and four girls be seated in a line so that a particular boy and a particular girl do not sit together?

(A) $6 \times 7!$

(B) $8! - 7!$

(C) $12 \times 7!$

(D) $3 \times 8!$

(E) $48 \times 7!$

Solve yourself:

34. A school examination consists of five questions, each having two parts. In how many ways can a student attempt at least one part of any of the questions?

(A) 624

(B) 625

(C) 1023

(D) 1024

(E) 4095

Solve yourself:

35. Given that

A = Number of ways 11 players can be selected out of 25 players, and

B = Number of ways 14 players can be selected out of 25 players

Which of the following statements is correct?

(A) $A = \dfrac{14}{11} \times B$

(B) $A = \dfrac{11}{14} \times B$

(C) $A = 3 \times B$

(D) $A = \dfrac{1}{3} \times B$

(E) $A = B$

Solve yourself:

36. Given that

A = Number of ways four marbles can be placed in three containers, and

B = Number of ways three marbles can be placed in four containers

Which of the following statements is correct?

(A) $A = \dfrac{3^4}{4^3} \times B$

(B) $A = \dfrac{4^3}{3^4} \times B$

(C) $A = \dfrac{3}{4} \times B$

(D) $A = \dfrac{4}{3} \times B$

(E) $A = B$

Solve yourself:

37. How many four digit numbers less than 2000 can be formed, using the digits '0', '1' and '2', with repetition of digits allowed?

    (A) 9

    (B) 12

    (C) 18

    (D) 27

    (E) 81

    Solve yourself:

38. In how many ways can a team of three members be selected from three men and two women so that at least one woman is always there in the team?

    (A) 3

    (B) 6

    (C) 9

    (D) 18

    (E) 27

    Solve yourself:

39. In how many ways can three boys and three girls be seated in a line so that the boys and girls sit in alternate positions?

(A) 3

(B) 6

(C) 12

(D) 36

(E) 72

Solve yourself:

40. In how many ways can four boys and three girls be seated on a circular table so that a particular boy and girl sit together?

(A) 120

(B) 240

(C) 600

(D) 720

(E) 1440

Solve yourself:

41. In how many ways can one mathematics book from six different mathematics books and one physics book from three identical physics books be selected?

(A) 1

(B) 3

(C) 6

(D) 9

(E) 18

Solve yourself:

42. In how many ways all the letters of the word LATTE can be arranged to form different words so that both T's are together?

(A) 10

(B) 12

(C) 18

(D) 24

(E) 48

Solve yourself:

43. In how many ways can five friends A, B, C, D and E stand for a photograph such that A stands immediately in front of D?

(A) 6

(B) 12

(C) 24

(D) 48

(E) 60

Solve yourself:

44. For how many four digit numbers, the digit '0' appears in the tens' position?

(A) 600

(B) 729

(C) 810

(D) 900

(E) 1000

Solve yourself:

45. In how many ways can one boy and one girl be selected from a group of three boys and two girls?

   (A) 2

   (B) 3

   (C) 6

   (D) 8

   (E) 9

   Solve yourself:

46. How many distinct words (meaningful or meaningless) can be formed using all the letters of the word "BANANA" ?

   (A) 9

   (B) 60

   (C) 120

   (D) 720

   (E) 900

   Solve yourself:

47. How many distinct words with or without meaning can be formed using all the letters of the word "BANANA" such that no two "Ns" come together?

(A) 10

(B) 20

(C) 30

(D) 40

(E) 50

Solve yourself:

48. How many spy-codes are possible taking all the symbols together with the following shapes such that no codes must have together the □ at the beginning and the ◊ at the end?

    □ ▷ ⊗ ⊘ ◊

(A) 20

(B) 60

(C) 84

(D) 114

(E) 120

Solve yourself:

49. Each participant in a certain study was assigned a sequence of 3 different letters from the set {A, B, C, D, E, F, G, H}. If no sequence was assigned to more than one participant and if 36 of the possible sequences were not assigned, what was the number of participants in the study? (Note, for example, that the sequence A, B, E is different from the sequence E, B, A).

(A) 20

(B) 92

(C) 300

(D) 372

(E) 476

50. Each signal that a certain ship can make is comprised of 3 different flags hanging vertically in a particular order. How many unique signals can be made if there are 4 different flags available?

    (A) 10

    (B) 12

    (C) 20

    (D) 24

    (E) 36

3.2 Data Sufficiency

Data sufficiency questions have five standard options. They are listed below and will not be repeated for each question.

(A) Statement (1) ALONE is sufficient, but statement (2) ALONE is not sufficient to answer the question asked.

(B) Statement (2) ALONE is sufficient, but statement (1) ALONE is not sufficient to answer the question asked.

(C) both the statements (1) and (2) TOGETHER are sufficient to answer the question asked, but NEITHER statement ALONE is sufficient to answer the question asked.

(D) EACH statement ALONE is sufficient to answer the question asked.

(E) Statements (1) and (2) TOGETHER are NOT sufficient to answer the question asked, and additional data specific to the problem are needed.

51. Group A of a soccer event has 8 teams. How many matches were played in group A?

   (1) Each team played other teams at least once.

   (2) Each team played at the most 8 matches.

   Solve yourself:

52. A man invites his p number of friends to a party. q number of friends do not turn up to the party. In how many ways can 5-member teams be formed?

   (1) Had there been 2 few members present in the party, it would have been possible to form 56 numbers of five-member teams.

   (2) $p = q + 10$.

   Solve yourself:

53. 4-digit numbers are formed using the digits p, q, r, and s, with none equals to 0. Repetition of digits is allowed. How many of these numbers would be even?

   (1) There are exactly 2 even digits among p, q, r, and s.

   (2) $p + q = r + s$.

   Solve yourself:

54. If a captain of a team has to select n players out of $(n + 2)$ players, what is the value of n?

   (1) The captain can select 2 players out of $(n + 2)$ players in 28 ways.

   (2) The captain can select all the players out of $(n + 2)$ players in 1 way.

   Solve yourself:

55.   8 points lie on a plane. How many different triangles can be drawn out of these points?

    (1)   There are exactly 4 co-linear points among 8 points.

    (2)   Fewer than 70 unique quadrilaterals can be formed out of these points.

Solve yourself:

56.   In how many ways can 2 boys and 2 girls be chosen from a class?

    (1)   There are as many boys as girls in the class.

    (2)   The number of ways 3 boys can be chosen equals the number of ways 3 girls can be chosen.

Solve yourself:

57.   Are there more than 8 balls is the box?

    (1)   The number of ways of selecting 1 ball equals 8 times the number of ways of selecting all the balls.

    (2)   The number of ways of selecting 3 balls equals the number of ways of selecting 5 balls.

Solve yourself:

58.   John is among few promising players in the school. In how many ways can 3 players be chosen for a tournament such that John is among the 3 players?

(1) The number of ways 3 players are chosen such that Harry, another player, is not chosen, and John is chosen is 15.

(2) The number of ways 3 players are chosen such that both Harry, and John are chosen is 6.

Solve yourself:

59. A group of 10 people comprises few Japanese, Australians, and Chinese. If 4 people are chosen at random from the group to form a committee, in how many ways can 2 people of them be Japanese?

(1) Number of Japanese equals that of Australians.

(2) Number of Chinese is less than 4.

Solve yourself:

60. A box contains 9 balls; they are either black, green, or yellow. 2 balls are drawn from the box at random. Are there equal number of balls of each color in the box?

(1) Number of black balls equals half the number of green and yellow balls combined.

(2) The ratio of number of ways both the balls drawn are of any color other than black to the number of ways both the balls drawn are black is 5.

Solve yourself:

61. How many students are there in the group?

(1) Number of ways three students can be selected to form a team is 35.

(2) Number of ways all the students can be selected to form a team is 1.

Solve yourself:

62. Does the bag contain more than 15 balls?

(1) Number of ways of selecting two balls equals 105 times the number of ways of selecting all the balls.

(2) Number of ways of selecting six balls equals the number of ways of selecting nine balls.

Solve yourself:

63. 4-digit numbers are formed using unique digits: $3, 4, 5, \& n$. What is the value of n if repetition of digits is allowed?

(1) There are thrice as many odd 4-digit numbers as even 4-digit numbers.

(2) n is non-prime.

Solve yourself:

64. How many three-digit numbers can be formed using only five unique digits from 0–9? Repetition of digits is allowed.

(1) The five unique digits include a digit that is divisible by other four digits.

(2) As many as 500 four-digit numbers can be formed using these five unique digits.

Solve yourself:

65. If there are 7 generals, and a team of few generals was formed, how many generals are there in the team?

(1) The number of generals in the team is such that it makes it possible to form teams with the highest number of ways.

(2) The number of generals in the team is such that if we increase the count of generals by one, it makes it possible to form teams with the highest number of ways.

Solve yourself:

Chapter 4

Answer Key

4.1 Problem Solving

(1) D	(18) B	(35) E
(2) D	(19) B	(36) A
(3) E	(20) D	(37) D
(4) B	(21) A	(38) C
(5) C	(22) C	(39) E
(6) C	(23) D	(40) B
(7) C	(24) D	(41) C
(8) C	(25) B	(42) D
(9) D	(26) C	(43) C
(10) D	(27) C	(44) D
(11) B	(28) B	(45) C
(12) D	(29) B	(46) B
(13) C	(30) C	(47) D
(14) D	(31) A	(48) D
(15) B	(32) C	(49) C
(16) B	(33) A	(50) D
(17) E	(34) C	

4.2 Data Sufficiency

(51) E

(52) D

(53) A

(54) A

(55) A

(56) E

(57) D

(58) D

(59) C

(60) E

(61) A

(62) D

(63) E

(64) D

(65) C

Chapter 5

Solutions

5.1 Problem Solving

1. For a 4-digit number to be even, its unit digit must be either 4 or 8.

    Number of ways, unit place can be filled = 2 (either 4 or 8)

    Number of ways, tenth place can be filled = 4; given that the repetition is allowed.

    Number of ways, hundredth place can be filled = 4

    Number of ways, thousandth place can be filled = 4

    So, total number of ways = 2.4.4.4 = 128 ways.

    The correct answer is option D.

2. Number of ways, each letter can be chosen = 26
    So, total number of ways of choosing 26 letters for three places = 26^3.

    Similarly, number of ways, each digit can be chosen = 10
    So, total number of ways of choosing 10 digits for three places = 10^3.

    These two blocks of the digits and the letters can be arranged in 2 ways (At the beginning or at the end).

    So, total number of ways = $2.26^3.10^3$ ways.

    The correct answer is option D.

3. '3' can be placed in the following ways in 5-digit numbers: 3XXXX, X3XXX, XX3XX, XXX3X, and XXXX3. Since '3' has to appear only once, we have 9 choices for each vacant place out of digits 0-9 (excluding the digit '3').

    But wait! A 5-digit number cannot begin with a digit '0', so the 5-digit numbers that do not begin with '3' will have only 8 number of ways to its fill ten-thousandth place.

    For numbers X3XXX, XX3XX, XXX3X, and XXXX3, total number of ways = $4.8.9^3$

    For number 3XXXX, total number of ways = 9^4

Hence, total number of ways $= 9^4 + 4.8.9^3$

The correct answer is option E.

4. We can start with the first key. After maximum 7 number of trials, we can conclude that the last key belongs to the 8th lock. Similarly, for the 2nd key, there would be 6 trails. So, in total trying with all keys, we will need $7 + 6 + 5 + 4 + 3 + 2 + 1 = 28$ trials.

The correct answer is option B.

5. Number of ways n players can be selected out of $(2n + 1)$ players:

$$C_n^{2n+1} = \frac{(2n + 1)!}{n!.(2n + 1 - n)!}$$
$$= \frac{(2n + 1)!}{n!.(n + 1)!} = 126 \text{ (Given)}$$

The better approach to get the value of n would be to plug in values from the options. We recommend that you follow a strategy on which option to try first while plugging in?

In the GMAT exam, if the option values are arranged in ascending order, follow B & D strategy while plugging in.

B & D strategy

(1) Plug in option B value first. If Right hand side (RHS) value matches the Left hand side (LHS) value, option B is the correct answer, else

(2) If the value derived (LHS) is more than the desired (RHS) value, option A could be the correct answer. Now plug in option A value, and check if Right hand side (RHS) value matches the Left hand side (LHS) value.

(3) If the value derived (LHS) is less than desired (RHS) value, option A and B cannot be the correct answers. Try option D instead of option C.

(4) If, for option D, Right hand side (RHS) value matches with the Left hand side (LHS) value, option D is the correct answer, else

(5) If the value derived (LHS) is more than desired (RHS) value, option C is the correct answer.

(6) If the value derived (LHS) is less than desired (RHS) value, option E is the correct answer.

Let us try with option B value, $n = 3$, we get $\dfrac{(2n + 1)!}{n!.(n + 1)!} = \dfrac{7!}{3!.4!} = 35$. Since the derived value (35) is less than the desired value (126), hence option B or A cannot be the correct answers.

Let us try with option D value, $n = 5$, we get $\dfrac{(2n+1)!}{n!.(n+1)!} = \dfrac{11!}{5!.6!} = 462$. Since the derived value (462) is more than the desired value (126), hence option C is the correct answer. We can mark the answer without even trying option C. For the sake of your curiosity, we present to you the value.

At $n = 4$, $\dfrac{(2n+1)!}{n!.(n+1)!} = \dfrac{9!}{4!.5!} = 126$ (desired value)

The correct answer is option C.

6. A triangle can be drawn taking any 3 vertices of a polygon.
   So, the number of triangles = $C_3^8 = \dfrac{8.7.6}{1.2.3} = 56$

   The correct answer is option C.

   A regular Octagon (8-sided polygon) will not have 3 or more number of co-linear vertices, hence there is no need to think of deducting a few number of dummy triangles formed out of co-linear points.

   What if the question had been:

   How many triangles are possible out of 8 points lying in a plane, out of which 4 points are co-linear?

   The answer would not be 56. There would be a few dummy triangles formed out of 4 co-linear points, and we must deduct those from 56.

   Number of dummy triangles = $C_3^4 = C_1^4 = 4$

   So, total number of genuine triangles = $56 - 4 = 52$ triangles

7. Number of ways of choosing 1 cube from Puzzle box1 = $C_1^{10} = 10$

   Number of ways of choosing 2 cubes from Puzzle box2 = $C_2^5 = \dfrac{5.4}{1.2} = 10$

   Total number of ways = $10.10 = 100$

   The correct answer is option C.

8. 'Numbers less than 1000' means all 1-digit, 2-digit and 3-digit numbers (1 to 999).

Number of ways of making 1-digit numbers out of 4 digits 3, 4, 5, and 6 = 4.

Number of ways of making 2-digit numbers out of 4 digits 3, 4, 5, and 6 = 4.4 = 16. (Remember that the repetition of digits is allowed. Questions does not restrict us to use the given digits once.)

Similarly, the number of ways of making 3-digit numbers out of 4 digits 3, 4, 5, and 6 = 4.4.4 = 64.

Total number of ways (Total 'numbers less than 1000') = 4 + 16 + 64 = 84.

The correct answer is option C.

9.   Number of ways of choosing 2 members from 5 individuals = $C_2^5 = \dfrac{5.4}{1.2} = 10$.

Since 2 specific individuals **together** must not be in the team, hence the number of ways 2 specific individuals can be chosen = 1.

Hence, the total number of ways = 10 − 1 = 9.

The correct answer is option D.

Remember that the question asks that the 2 specific individuals **together** must not be in the team, however one of them alone can be a part of the team.

Had you excluded both the individuals while calculating the number of ways, you could have wrongly calculated the answer as $C_2^3 = C_1^3 = 3$.

10.   Number of ways of choosing 2 boys out of 10 boys = $C_2^{10} = \dfrac{10.9}{1.2} = 45$

Number of ways of choosing 2 girls out of 12 girls = $C_2^{12} = \dfrac{12.11}{1.2} = 66$

Hence, the total number of ways = $45 \times 66 = 2970$.

The correct answer is option D.

11.   Number of ways the first place of 5-letter word can be filled (Only vowels) = 5.

Number of ways the second place of 5-letter word can be filled = 26. Remember that the second, third and fourth place can be filled with any letter. **Not only**

consonants!

Number of ways the third place of 5-letter word can be filled = 26.

Number of ways the fourth place of 5-letter word can be filled = 26.

Number of ways the fifth place of 5-letter word can be filled (Only vowels) = 5.

Total number of ways = $5^2.26^3$

The correct answer is option B.

12. Number of ways 5 letters can be chosen for 5 places = 5^5

Let us calculate how many 5 letter codes start from *muc _ _*?

To get that, fix first 3 places with letters *m, u, & c.* So, the number of ways 5-letter can be chosen for remaining 2 places = 5^2

Hence, the total number of desired ways = $5^5 - 5^2$

The correct answer is option D.

13. Number of ways he can answer each question = 2
     Hence, the number of ways he can answer 3 questions = 2.2.2 = 8

     Number of ways he can speak truth for each question = 1
     So, the number of ways he can speak truth for 3 questions = 1.1.1 = 1

     Hence, number of ways he can hide the truth = 8 − 1 = 7

     The correct answer is option C.

14. Number of ways 3 cubes can be chosen = $C_3^5 = \dfrac{5.4}{1.2} = 10$

     Number of ways 3 chosen cubes can be arranged to present unique pattern = 3! = 3.2.1 = 6

     Hence, total number of ways = 10.6 = 60

     The correct answer is option D.

This question can be solved alternatively.

Number of ways 3 cubes can be chosen and arranged = $P_3^5 = 5.4.3 = 60$

15. We know that if there are total n objects, out of these there are p number of one type of identical objects, q number of another type of identical objects, and r number of another type of identical objects, then the number of ways these objects can be arranged in a row to have unique patterns = $\dfrac{n!}{p!.q!.r!}$

   There are total 9 letters "APPEALING"; so $n = 9$, and there are 2 Ps and 2 As, so $p = 2$, and $q = 2$.
   Thus, the answer is $\dfrac{9!}{2!.2!}$.

   The correct answer is option A.

16. Treat L and G as a single object. Though there are total 9 letters, this would imply that there are 8 objects to be arranged in a line. So the total number of words would be $\dfrac{8!}{2!.2!}$. (2 Ps, and 2 As)

   However, L and G could interchange their positions as 'LG' or 'GL' in 2! ways. Thus, the correct answer is $2! \times \left[\dfrac{8!}{2!.2!}\right] = \dfrac{8!}{2!}$

   The correct answer is option B.

17. There are 4 vowels (A, A, E, and I) and 5 consonants (P, P, L, N, and G). Treating the vowels as one object, there would be total 6 objects to be arranged in a line. This can be done in $\dfrac{6!}{2!}$ ways (2 P's) and the vowels can be arranged in $\dfrac{4!}{2!}$ ways (2 A's). Thus, the number of ways = $\dfrac{6!}{2!} \times \dfrac{4!}{2!} = 4320$.

   The correct answer is option E.

18. Number of ways 11 students of out 15 can be selected
   $= C_{11}^{15} = C_{(15-11)}^{15} = C_4^{15} = \dfrac{15.14.13.12}{1.2.3.4} = 1365$

   Note: $C_r^n = C_{n-r}^n$

   It is important that the arrangement of 11 students must be ignored as the question states that the order of selection does not matter.

   The correct answer is option B.

19. Number of ways 2 generals from 5 UK generals can be selected = $C_2^5 = \dfrac{5.4}{1.2} = 10$

Number of ways 3 generals from 6 French generals can be selected = $C_3^6 = \dfrac{6.5.4}{1.2.3} = 20$

Total number of ways = 10.20 = 200

The correct answer is option B.

20. Number of ways 2 actors from soaps can be selected = $C_2^5 = \dfrac{5.4}{1.2} = 10$

Number of ways 3 actors from reality shows can be selected = $C_3^8 = \dfrac{8.7.6}{1.2.3} = 56$

Total number of ways = 10.56 = 560

The correct answer is option D.

21. Since the captain is to be chosen, the number of players left to be chosen = 15-1 = 14.

Again since the captain is already chosen and the injured player is not to be chosen, number of players left for selection = 17 − 1 − 1 = 15.

Number of ways 14 players can be selected out of 15 players = $C_{14}^{15} = C_1^{15} = 15$.
Note:- $C_r^n = C_{n-r}^n$

The correct answer is option A.

22. Number of ways 3 elements can be selected out of 5 elements = $C_3^5 = \dfrac{5.4.3}{1.2.3} = 10$.

Since the sub-set {A, C, D} is to be excluded, hence the required number of sets = 10 − 1 = 9. Note that in a set, the order or the arrangement of the elements is immaterial.

The correct answer is option C.

23. Number of ways 1 male can be selected for the group1 = 10.
Number of ways 1 female can be selected for the group1 = 8.

Hence, total number of ways, 1 male and 1 female can be selected for the group1 = 10.8 = 80.

Similarly,

Number of ways 1 male can be selected for the group2 = 9 (since one male is already selected for group1.)
Number of ways 1 female can be selected for the group1 = 7. (One female is already selected for group1.)

Hence, total number of ways 1 male and 1 female can be selected for the group2 = 9.7 = 63.

Now, which pair of dancers will join which group is not specified as group numbers are not fixed. So, if we do 80 × 63 = 5040 ways, we will get an ordered selection which is incorrect. Since there are two groups, the answer should be 5040/2! = 2520.

The correct answer is option D.

Alternate approach:

We can select 2 males for the groups in $C_2^{10} = 45$ ways.
We can select 2 females for the groups in $C_2^8 = 28$ ways.

Let us say the males are M1, M2 and the females are F1, F2. These 4 people can be grouped in 2 ways: (M1F1 and M2F2) or (M1F2 and M2F1).

Thus, the answer is: 45 × 28 × 2 = 2520.

Had you done this way—Total no. of ways = $C_2^{10}.C_2^8 = 1260$, it would have been wrong since the question asks for 1 male and 1 female for each group, but 1260 represents selection of 2 males and 2 females. This means 4 dancers for only one group.

24. **Selection 1:** 4 batsmen, 6 bowlers, and 1 wicket-keeper

   Number of ways = $C_4^8.C_6^6.C_1^2 = C_4^8.C_0^6.C_1^2 = \left(\dfrac{8.7.6.5}{1.2.3.4}\right).1.2 = 140.$
   Note:- $C_r^n = C_{n-r}^n$ and $C_0^n = 1$

   Selection 2: 5 batsmen, 5 bowlers, and 1 wicket-keeper

Number of ways = $C_5^8.C_5^6.C_1^2 = C_3^8.C_1^6.C_1^2 = \left(\dfrac{8.7.6}{1.2.3}\right).6.2 = 672.$

Selection 3: 6 batsmen, 4 bowlers, and 1 wicket-keeper

Number of ways = $C_6^8.C_4^6.C_1^2 = C_2^8.C_2^6.C_1^2 = \left(\dfrac{8.7}{1.2}\right).\left(\dfrac{6.5}{1.2}\right).2 = 840.$

Hence, total number of ways = $140 + 672 + 840 = 1652$.

The correct answer is option D.

25. The person can choose one out of four salads in four ways and one topping out of six toppings in six ways.

    Thus, total number of ways of selecting a salad AND a topping = $4 \times 6 = 24$.

    The correct answer is option B.

26. The condition is: the string of the last three digits should not start nor end in '0'.

    Thus, the first of the last three digits can be filled using digits from '1' to '9' i.e. 9 ways (excluding '0').
    The second of the last three digits can be filled using digits from '0' to '9' i.e. 10 ways (including '0').
    The third of the last three digits can be filled using digits from '1' to '9' i.e. 9 ways (excluding '0').

    Thus, the number of possible telephone numbers = $9 \times 10 \times 9 = 810$.

    The correct answer is option C.

27. We can select three men from four in $C_3^4 = 4$ ways.

    We can select two women from three in $C_2^3 = 3$ ways.

    Thus, we can select three men AND two women in $C_3^4 \times C_2^3 = 4 \times 3 = 12$ ways.

    The correct answer is option C.

28. To make a three-digit number, we need to fill up three blank positions using the above digits.

Since the number should be even, the last digit should be '0' or '2'.

Case I: The last digit is '0': _ _ <u>0</u>

The first place can be filled using any of '2', '3','5' in three ways.
The second place can be filled in one less way (since repetition is not allowed) i.e. 2 ways.

Thus, we can have $3 \times 2 = 6$ such numbers.

Case II: The last digit is '2': _ _ <u>2</u>

The first place can be filled using any of '3' or '5' in two ways (since '0' cannot be used in the first place).
The second place can be filled in two ways (since zero can be used) i.e. two ways.

Thus, we can have $2 \times 2 = 4$ such numbers.

Thus, total # of such numbers = 6 + 4 = 10.

The correct answer is option B.

29. John can invite one friend in C_1^4 ways.

He can similarly invite two or three or all four friends in C_2^4, C_3^4 and C_4^4 ways respectively.

Thus, number of ways of doing this = $C_1^4 + C_2^4 + C_3^4 + C_4^4 = 4 + 6 + 4 + 1 = 15$.

Alternatively, we can say that John has two options for each friend: either to call him or not to call him.

Thus, total number of choices with John = $2 \times 2 \times 2 \times 2 = 16$.

This includes a case when John invites 'none'. Thus, we need to remove that possibility.

Hence, total ways = $2^4 - 1 = 15$.

The correct answer is option B.

30. Since AND must remain intact, we consider it as a single unit. We thus have four objects to be arranged in a circle: (R), (AND), (O) and (M).

This can be done in (4 - 1)! = 3! = 6 ways.

The correct answer is option C.

31. INDIANA consists of seven letters of which two are Is, two are Ns and two are As.

Thus, the number of ways in which the letters can be arranged

$$= \frac{7!}{2!2!2!} = \frac{7 \times 6 \times 5 \times 4 \times 3 \times 2 \times 1}{8} = 7 \times 6 \times 5 \times 3 = 630.$$

The correct answer is option A.

32. First we need to select five members from the eight probable members in $C_5^8 = C_3^8$ ways.

Then we need to decide the speaker from the selected five members in C_1^5 ways.

Thus, total number of ways of selecting the team AND deciding the speaker

$$= C_3^8 \times C_1^5 = \frac{8!}{5!.3!} \times 5 = \frac{8!}{4!.3!} = \frac{8 \times 7 \times 6 \times 5 \times 4!}{4!.3!} = 8 \times 7 \times 5 = 280.$$

The correct answer is option C.

33. Let us find the total number of arrangements without any constraint.

Eight people can be seated in 8! ways.

Let us find the number of cases when the particular boy and girl sit together.

We group the two of them as one unit. This results in seven units to be arranged in a line.

Thus can be arranged in 7! ways.

But, for each of the above arrangements, the boy and girl can interchange positions between themselves in 2! ways.

Thus, total number of ways = 7! × 2!

Thus, the number of ways when the boy and girl do not sit together

$$= 8! - 7! \times 2! = 7!(8 - 2) = 6 \times 7!$$

The correct answer is option A.

34. The student has four options for each question: attempt both parts, attempt only the first part, attempt only the second part or leave the question entirely.

Since there are five questions each having four options, total possible options for the student $= 4 \times 4 \times 4 \times 4 \times 4 = 4^5$.

Out of these, there is one option where he does not attempt anything which we need to ignore.

Thus, number of possible ways $= 4^5 - 1 = 2^{10} - 1 = 1024 - 1 = 1023$.

The correct answer is option C.

35. Since the question asks for calculating the number of ways of selecting, we will apply 'Combination' and not 'Permutation'.

We know that, number of ways of selecting r objects out of n objects $= C_r^n = \dfrac{n!}{r!.\,(n-r)!}$

A = # of ways 11 players can be selected out of 25 players $= C_{11}^{25} = \dfrac{25!}{11!.\,(14)!}$

B = # of ways 14 players can be selected out of 25 players $= C_{14}^{25} = \dfrac{25!}{14!.\,(11)!}$

As we see that A and B are equal in value, there is no need to calculate the values.

The correct answer is option E.

36. Since the question asks for calculating the number of ways of assigning marbles to containers, we will apply 'Permutation' since there can be different ways of assigning marbles to containers.

We know that, number of ways of assigning r objects in n places $= n^r$

A = # of ways four marbles can be placed in three containers $= 3^4$.

B = # of ways three marbles can be placed in four containers = 4^3.

Thus, $A = \dfrac{3^4}{4^3} \times B$

The correct answer is option A.

37. Since the question asks for calculating the # of numbers formed using digits, we will apply 'Permutation' since for the same digits, many numbers can be formed by changing the positions of the digits.

Since four digit numbers are to be formed, we need to fill up four blank positions:
_ _ _ _ .

The first position can be filled up in one way (only possible digit is '1' since the number should be less than 2000).

The second, third and fourth positions can be filled up in three ways each (since each of '0', '1', and '2' can be used).

Thus, total # of such numbers = $1 \times 3 \times 3 \times 3 = 27$.

The correct answer is option D.

38. Since the question asks for calculating the number of ways of selecting, we will apply 'Combination' and not 'Permutation'.

We know that, number of ways of selecting r objects out of n objects = $C_r^n = \dfrac{n!}{r!\,(n-r)!}$

Since at least one woman needs to be a part of the team, we have two cases:

   1. Only one woman (from two) and two men (from three): $C_1^2 \times C_2^3 = 2 \times 3 = 6$ ways

   2. Both women (from two) and one man (from three): $C_2^2 \times C_1^3 = 1 \times 3 = 3$ ways

Thus, we have a total of = 6 + 3 = 9 ways.

The correct answer is option C.

39. Since the question asks for calculating the seating arrangements, we will apply 'Permutation'.

We know that, # of ways of arranging n objects in a line $= n!$

The boys and girls can sit in alternate positions in either of the two ways:

1. B G B G B G

2. G B G B G B

The three boys and the three girls can be separately arranged in their positions among themselves in $3! = 6$ ways each

Thus, total number of ways for each of the cases $= 6 \times 6 = 36$ ways.

Thus, total number of ways $= 36 \times 2 = 72$ ways.

The correct answer is option E.

40. Since the question asks for calculating the seating arrangements, we will apply 'Permutation'.

We know that, # of ways of arranging n objects in a circle $= (n - 1)!$

We group the particular boy and girl together. Thus, we now have 6 things to arrange in a circle: three boys, two girls and the boy-girl pair.

This can be done in $(6 - 1)! = 5! = 120$ ways.

For each such way, the boy and girl can interchange positions.

Thus, total ways $= 120 \times 2 = 240$.

The correct answer is option B.

41. Since the question asks for calculating the number of ways of selecting, we will apply 'Combination' and not 'Permutation'.

We know that, number of ways of selecting r objects out of n objects $= C_r^n = \dfrac{n!}{r!.\,(n-r)!}$

Number of ways of selecting one mathematics book from six different books = C_1^6 = 6 ways.

Number of ways of selecting one physics book from three identical books = 1 way (since there is nothing to choose if the objects are identical; thus, number of identical objects is immaterial.).

Thus, there are a total of $6 \times 1 = 6$ ways.

The correct answer is option C.

42. Since the question asks for calculating the number of ways of forming different words, we will apply 'Permutation' since there can be different ways of arranging the letters of a word to form new words.

Since both T's are to be kept together, we group them as one unit. Thus, there are four things to be arranged.

This can be done in 4! = 24 ways (here, we do not consider the interchanging positions of the two T's since they are identical and hence even on interchanging would give rise to the same situation).

The correct answer is option D.

43. Since the question asks for calculating the number of ways the friends can stand in a line, we will apply 'Permutation'.

We know that, # of ways of arranging n objects in a line = $n!$

Since A stands immediately in front of D, we group A and D as one unit (AD).

Thus, there are four things to be arranged in a line.

This can be done in 4! = 24 ways (here we do not consider the interchanging of A and D since A has to stand in front of D).

The correct answer is option C.

44. Since the question asks for calculating the # of numbers, we will apply 'Permutation' since different numbers can be formed by rearranging the same digits.

In a four digit number, we need to fill up four blanks: _ _ _ _.

Of these, the tens' position has '0'.

The thousands' position can be filled in 9 ways (since the digit '0' cannot be used, as doing so will render 3 digit numbers), the hundreds' position can be filled in 10 ways, and the units' position can be filled in 10 ways.

So, the number of four digit numbers with '0' in the tens' place is $9 \times 10 \times 10 = 900$.

The correct answer is option D.

45. Since the question asks for calculating the number of ways of selecting, we will apply 'Combination' and not 'Permutation'.

We know that, # of ways of selecting r objects out of n objects = $C_r^n = \dfrac{n!}{r!.(n-r)!}$

We can select one boy from three boys in $C_1^3 = 3$ ways.

We can select one girl from two girls in $C_1^2 = 2$ ways.

Since we need to select one boy AND one girl, total number of ways = $3 \times 2 = 6$ ways.

The correct answer is option C.

46. We know that if there are total n objects, out of these there are p number of one type of identical objects, q number of another type of identical objects, and r number of another type of identical objects, then the number of ways these objects can be arranged in a row to have unique patterns = $\dfrac{n!}{p!.q!.r!}$

There are a total 6 letters in BANANA; so $n = 6$, and there are 3 As and 2 Ns, so $p = 3$, and $q = 2$.

Thus, the answer is $\dfrac{6!}{3!.2!} = 60$.

The correct answer is option B.

47. We know that if there are total n objects, out of these there are p number of one type of identical objects, q number of another type of identical objects, and r number of another type of identical objects, then the number of ways these objects can be arranged in a row to have unique patterns = $\dfrac{n!}{p!.q!.r!}$

There are a total 6 letters in BANANA; there are 3 As and 2 Ns; since 2 'Ns' have to be together, let's consider them as one letter, thus, we have so $n = 6 - 1 = 5$, and $p = 3$.

Thus, the number of ways 2 'Ns' come together = $\dfrac{5!}{3!} = 20$.

But we are interested in finding out the number of ways 2 "Ns" do not come together.

Thus, the number of ways 2 'Ns' do not come together = total number of ways without any condition – the number of ways 2 'Ns' come together

Total number of ways without any condition = $\dfrac{6!}{3!.2!} = 60$.

Thus, the number of ways 2 'Ns' do not come together = 60 - 20 = 40.

The correct answer is option D.

48. There are a total of 5 symbols and we have take all of them together to form codes, considering that the □ must NOT be at the beginning and the ◊ must NOT be at the end of the codes.

Number of ways 5 symbols can be arranged = $P_5^5 = 5! = 120$. We will deduct the number of codes which starts the □ with and ends with the ◊; thus this asks for the arrangement of 3 symbols.

Number of ways 3 symbols can be arranged = $P_3^3 = 3! = 6$.

Thus, the desired number of codes = $120 - 6 = 114$.

The correct answer is option D.

49. Each person is assigned a sequence of three different letters from the set of 8 letters:
{A, B, C, D, E, F, G, H}.

Also, the order of the letters in a sequence differentiates one sequence from the other.

Number of ways of selecting 3 letters from the 8 letters = C_3^8

$$= \frac{8 \times 7 \times 6}{3 \times 2 \times 1} = 56$$

The number of ways the order of the letters can be decided for the same three letters

= Number of ways 3 letters can be arranged in a line

$= 3 \times 2 \times 1 = 6$

Thus, total number of distinct sequences = $56 \times 6 = 336$

Alternately, we have:

The total number of sequences formed = P_3^8

$= 8 \times 7 \times 6 = 336$

Since 36 of the sequences were not assigned, number of participants

$= 336 - 36 = 300$

The correct answer is option C.

50. Number of ways in which we can select and arrange 3 flags from the 4 available flags = P_3^4

$$= \frac{4!}{(4-3)!}$$

$= 4 \times 3 \times 2 \times 1$

$= 24$

Alternate approach:

We need to use 3 different flags in different orders to create a signal.

The first place can be filled from the 4 available flags in 4 ways.

The second place can be filled from the $(4 - 1) = 3$ remaining flags in 3 ways.

The third place can be filled from the $(3 - 1) = 2$ remaining flags in 2 ways.

Thus, total number of ways $= 4 \times 3 \times 2 = 24$

The correct answer is option D.

5.2 Data Sufficiency

51. From statement 1:

From statement 1, we know that the minimum number of matches played would be $(8 \times 7)/2 = 28$ matches (Each team plays minimum 7 matches; two teams play in a match), but each team could have played more number of matches. So, statement 1 is insufficient.

The correct answer would be either B, C, or E.

From statement 2:

It means that the maximum number of matches would be $(8 \times 8)/2 = 32$. We still do not know the unique answer. So, statement 2 is also sufficient.

The correct answer would be either C or E.

Thus, from both the statements together:

Even combining both the statements will not give the unique answer as the number of matches played can be anything between 28 and 32. Few teams could have played 7 matches each, while others may have played 8 matches each. We still do not know the unique answer.

The correct answer is option E.

52. Presently there are $(p - q)$ members in the party, so the possible five-member teams $= C_5^{(p-q)}$. If we know the value of $(p - q)$, we get the answer.

From statement 1:

From statement 1, we know that $C_5^{(p-q-2)} = 56$.

Since right hand side = 56 is a finite value, we can surely get the value of $(p - q - 2)$. There is no need to calculate the value of $(p - q - 2)$, as in DS, we need to be satisfied if there is going to be a unique answer. So, statement 1 is sufficient.

The correct answer would be either A or D.

For your curiosity, $C_5^8 = 56 \Rightarrow p - q - 2 = 8 \Rightarrow p - q = 10$; there were $C_5^{10} = 252$ ways of forming the teams.

From statement 2:

If $p = q + 10$, then $p - q = 10$, and $C_5^{(p-q)} = C_5^{10}$. Again a finite value! So, statement 2 is also sufficient.

The correct answer is option D.

53. From statement 1:

For a 4 digit-number to be even, its unit digit must be Even. From statement 1, we know that there are exactly 2 even digits, so the other 2 digits would be odd. This information itself is sufficient to conclude that statement 1 alone is sufficient to answer the question.

However, we calculate the number of ways to get the answer.

Number of ways, unit place can be filled = 2;
Number of ways, tenth place can be filled = 4; given that the repetition is allowed.
Number of ways, hundredth place can be filled = 4;
Number of ways, thousandth place can be filled = 4;

So, total number of ways = 2.4.4.4 = 128 ways.

The correct answer would be either A or D.

From statement 2:

Statement 2 is insufficient as Even + Even = Odd + Odd or Even + Odd = Even + Odd, implying that the two digits among digits p, q, r, and s can be even, and the two digits can be odd; whereas Odd + Odd = Odd + Odd or Even + Even = Even + Even, implying that all the digits p, q, r, and s can be either Odd or Even. Depending on the number of Even digits and Odd digits, the number of 4-digit even numbers would change.

See how: $0 + 8 = 3 + 5$; $1 + 7 = 3 + 5$; and $2 + 8 = 4 + 6$. There is no unique answer.

The correct answer is option A.

54. From statement 1:

The meaning of statement 1 is that $C_2^{n+2} = 28 \Rightarrow \dfrac{(n+2)(n+1)}{1.2} = 28 \Rightarrow$ $(n+2)(n+1) = 56$. 56 is a product of two consecutive numbers; the numbers must be 7 & 8.

$\Rightarrow n + 2 = 8$ and $n + 1 = 7 \Rightarrow n=6$. So, statement 1 is sufficient.

The correct answer would be either A or D.

From statement 2:

This statement does not add any value. It simply means that $C_{n+2}^{n+2} = 1$. We cannot get the value of n.

The correct answer is option A.

55. A triangle can be drawn taking any 3 points on a plane. So, the number of triangles = $C_3^8 = \dfrac{8.7.6}{1.2.3} = 56$. It seems that the question stem is sufficient to answer the question. On a funny side, it appears as if no statement is needed, but by looking at statement 1, we understand that there may be few co-linear points, forming a few dummy triangles, and thus the actual number of unique triangles may be less than 56.

From statement 1:

Simply knowing that exactly 4 co-linear points lie on the plane, we can calculate the exact number of unique triangles, so, statement 1 itself is sufficient.

The 56 triangles include the dummy triangles formed out of 4 collinear points, which are basically straight lines, so we must deduct these straight lines, so the actual triangles = $56 - C_3^4 = 56 - C_1^4 = 56 - 4 = 52$.

The correct answer would be either A or D.

From statement 2:

If no three or more points on the plane are collinear, then the possible quadrilaterals = $C_4^8 = \dfrac{8.7.6.5}{1.2.3.4} = 70$. This information itself in not sufficient. This leads to a possibility of having at least one to many collinear points. The statement is not sufficient.

The correct answer is option A.

56. To answer the question, we must know how many boys and girls are there in the class.

From statement 1:

The statement is clearly insufficient as we do not know how many boys and girls are there in the class.

The correct answer would be either B, C, or E.

From statement 2:

The statement is also insufficient as we do not know how many boys and girls are there in the class. Merely knowing 'the number of ways 3 boys can be chosen equals the number of ways 3 girls can be chosen' is same as knowing that there are as many boys as girls in the class, which is given in statement 1.

The correct answer would be either C or E.

Thus, from both the statements together:

Even after combining both the statements, we cannot get the answer as both the statements are basically rephrased version of each other.

The correct answer is option E.

57. From statement 1:

Say, the number of balls is n, so as per the statement, $C_1^n = 8.C_n^n => n = 8.1 = 8$.

So, there are exactly 8 balls, not more. The answer is a 'No'—a unique answer. So, statement 1 alone is sufficient.

The correct answer would be either A or D.

From statement 2:

As per the statement $=> C_3^n = C_5^n$

$=> C_{(n-3)}^n = C_5^n$; we know that $C_r^n = C_{(n-r)}^n$

$=> n - 3 = 5$

$=> n = 8$

Again, there are exactly 8 balls, not more. The answer is 'No'—a unique answer. So, statement 2 alone is also sufficient.

The correct answer is option D.

Alternate approach:

If the number of ways of selecting r objects equals the number of ways of selecting s objects, then the total number of objects equals $(r + s)$. So, in our case $n = 3 + 5 = 8$ balls.

58. From statement 1:

Say, the number of players is n. If Harry is not chosen and John is already chosen, then the number of players available for selection is $(n - 2)$, and the number of players to be selected equals $3 - 1 = 2$ (John is already chosen).

So, the number of such ways = $C_2^{(n-2)} = 15$

$=> \dfrac{(n - 2).(n - 3)}{1.2} = 15$

$=> (n - 2).(n - 3) = 30.$

You just not solve a quadratic equation to get the value of n. See the alternate approach: '30' is a product of two consecutive numbers: 5 & 6, so $n - 2 = 6$ or $n = 8$. Once we know the value of n, we can be sure that we can get the answer. There is no need to calculate the value.

However, for your curiosity, we calculate the ways, 3 players can be chosen for the tournament such that John is among 3 players = $C_{(3-1)}^7 = C_2^7 = 21$ ways. So, statement 1 alone is sufficient.

The correct answer would be either A or D.

From statement 2:

Similarly, if Harry and John are chosen, then the number of players available for selection is $(n - 2)$, and players to be selected equals $3 - 2 = 1$ (Harry and John are chosen).

So, the number of ways of selecting one player = $C_1^{n-2} = 6 => n - 2 = 6 => n = 8$. Again, we get the value of number of players, and hence we can calculate the ways, 3 players can be chosen for the tournament such that John is among 3 players the way we did in statement 1. So, statement 2 alone is also sufficient.

The correct answer is option D.

59.   From statement 1:

This statement itself is insufficient as there could be many possible combinations considering all the possibilities. So, statement 1 alone is insufficient.

The correct answer would be either B, C, or E.

From statement 2:

Number of Chinese (less than 4) can be either 3, 2, or 1, but we do not know anything about the number of Japanese, and the number of Australians. So, statement 2 alone is insufficient.

The correct answer would be either C or E.

Thus, from both the statements together:

If the number of Chinese are either 3, 2, or 1, and number of Japanese equals that of Australians, then the number of Chinese can only be in Even number as the Odd value will result in a fractional number for number of Japanese and the number of Australians. Let us see how.

=> Number of Chinese + Number of Japanese + Number of Australians = 10;

Say Number of Japanese = Number of Australians = x.

=> Assume that the number of Chinese is an Odd number = 3.

=> $10 = 3 + 2x => x = 3.5$.

So, if the number of Chinese is an Odd number, number of Japanese, and number of Australians would be a fraction, which is not possible.

So, Number of Chinese = 2 (Only even number among 1, 2, & 3), hence Number of Japanese = Number of Australians = 4 each.

We now know the finite values of the number of each national, so we can get the unique answer. There is no need to calculate the answer in most DS questions.

The correct answer is option C.

We calculate the answer for your curiosity.

Number of ways, 4 people can be chosen such that 2 of them are Japanese

= [Number of ways 2 Japanese (total 4) chosen] × [Number of ways 2 are chosen out of Chinese (total 2) and Australians (total 4)]

$$= C_2^4 . C_2^6 = \left[\frac{4.3}{1.2} \right] . \left[\frac{6.5}{1.2} \right] = 90 \text{ ways.}$$

60. From statement 1:

Say the number of green and yellow balls combined = n, then the number of black balls = $n/2$. So, $n/2 + n = 9 => n = 6$, and $n/2 = 3$. This statement is clearly insufficient; though we know that the number of black balls is 3, we are not sure whether green, and yellow balls are 3 each.

The correct answer would be either B, C, or E.

From statement 2:

Given that: $\dfrac{\text{Number of ways both the balls drawn are either green or yellow}}{\text{Number of ways both the balls drawn are black}} = 5$

Say the number of green and yellow balls combined = n, then the number of black balls = $9 - n$.

So, $\dfrac{C_2^n}{C_2^{(9-n)}} = 5 => \dfrac{n.(n-1)}{(9-n)(8-n)} = 5.$

There is no need to solve the equation. Hit and Trial is the best approach. For $n = 6$, we get the solution. So, again, the number of green and yellow balls combined = 6, and number of black balls = 3; however like statement 1, we are not sure whether green, and yellow balls are 3 each .

The correct answer would be either C, or E.

Thus, from both the statements together:

Even after combing both the statements will not give us the answer as both the statements convey the same information.

The correct answer is option E.

61. From statement 1:

Say there are n number of students in the group, thus, the number of ways 3 students can be selected to form a team $= {}_3^n c = \dfrac{n.(n-1).(n-2)}{1.2.3} = 35$

$=> n.(n-1).(n-2) = 35.1.2.3 = 210$

Though it is difficult to calculate the value of n, it is not required till we are sure that we get a unique value of n; in this case, we see that 210 is a multiple of three consecutive numbers, thus n is a unique value.

So, statement 1 is sufficient. The correct answer would be A and D.

We can calculate the value of n, let us see how.

Since $n.(n-1).(n-2) = 210 = 2.3.5.7$, which is a multiple of four integers, thus we must make these four integers as three integers.

Let us do some hit and trial.

$2.3.5.7 = 6.5.7 = 2.15.7 = 3.5.14$, and so on; we see that by writing $2.3.5.7$ as $5.6.7$, we have multiples of three integers, thus $n = 7$.

From statement 2:

Since for any number of students, the number of ways to select all is 1, be it $n = 7, 8, 10....$ Thus this information is of no use.

Note that ${}_n^n c = 1$; we can never get the value of n.

Hence, statement 2 alone is not sufficient.

The correct answer is option A.

62. From statement 1:

Say number of balls = n, thus

$=> C_2^n = 105.C_n^n$

$=> \dfrac{n(n-1)}{2} = 105.1$

$=> n(n-1) = 210$

$=> n^2 - n - 210 = 0$

$=> n^2 - 15n + 14n - 210 = 0$

$=> n(n-15) + 14(n-15) = 0$

$=> (n-15)(n+14) = 0$

$=> n = 15$, as n cannot be negative—answer is No.

The statement is sufficient.

The correct answer would be either A or D.

From statement 2:

Given that,

$=> C_6^n = C_9^n$

$=> C_{n-6}^n = C_9^n$; since $C_r^n = C_{n-r}^n$

$=> n - 6 = 9$

$=> n = 15$—answer is No.

The statement is sufficient.

The correct answer is option D.

63. Since the digits are unique, n can be one among: $0, 1, 2, 6, 7, 8,$ & 9.

The meaning of 'repetition of digits is allowed' is that though digits: $3, 4, 5,$ & n are unique, each digit can be used more than once in numbers.

From statement 1:

Since the number of even numbers and the number of odd numbers are NOT equal, this implies that n cannot be one among: $0, 2, 6,$ & 8 even digits; if we have n as one among: $0, 2, 6,$ & 8, there would be two even and two odd digits, and this will render equal number of even and odd numbers.

Thus, n can only be one among: $1, 7,$ & 9

Since any of $1, 7,$ & 9 for n will make the statement true, we cannot get the unique value of n.

Statement 1 is not sufficient to answer the question.

The correct answer would be among B, C, and E.

From statement 2:

The statement is clearly not sufficient as n can have any value from $1, 6, 8,$ & 9.

Statement 2 is not sufficient to answer the question.

The correct answer would be between C and E.

Thus, from both the statements together:

Combining both the statement cannot help as now n can be either 1 or 9—No unique answer. Note that 1 is non-prime.

The correct answer is option E.

64. Number of 3-digit numbers formed out of five non-zero digits $= 5^3 = 125$; however if one of the digit is '0', total numbers would be $= 4.5^2 = 100$

Thus the question reduces to know whether one of the five digits is '0'.

From statement 1:

There is only one digit among all the digits that is divisible by all other nine digits and it is '0'; Digits 6 & 8 are divisible only by three digits other than itself, thus one of the five digits is '0'.

Statement 1 is sufficient to answer the question.

The correct answer would be between A and D.

From statement 2:

Number of 4-digit numbers formed out of five digits, excluding '0' = $4.5^3 = 500$; thus it also confirms that '0' is one of the five digits.

Statement 2 is sufficient to answer the question.

The correct answer is option D.

65. Say there are r number of generals in the team, thus total number of ways of forming team = C_r^7.

r can range from 1 to 7. We have to find the value of r.

From statement 1:

The meaning of statement 1: *The number of generals in the team is such that it makes it possible to form teams with the highest number of ways.* is that for $r = 1$ to 7, C_r^7 is the highest possible value. Or, in a simpler way, we have to find: which among $C_1^7, C_2^7, C_3^7, C_4^7, C_5^7, C_6^7,$ & C_7^7 is highest?

Note that in case of combination (not for permutation), as we increase the value of r, the value of C_r^n keeps on increasing, starting from 1, then after touching the highest value, it reduces to 1.

If n is an even number, C_r^n is highest for $r = \frac{n}{2}$; however if it is odd, we have would have two peaks: one at $r = \frac{n-1}{2}$ and one at one at $r = \frac{n+1}{2}$.

Note that for permutation, value of P_r^n, starting from 1, keeps on increasing, and ends at $n!$.

In the question, $n = 7$ is an odd number, thus we have two peak values: one at $r = \dfrac{7-1}{2} = 3$ and one at one at $r = \dfrac{7+1}{2} = 4$ or at $r = 3$ or 4—no unique value of r.

Let us see this.

- $C_0^7 = 1$

- $C_1^7 = 7$

- $C_2^7 = \dfrac{7.6}{1.2} = 21$

- $C_3^7 = \dfrac{7.6.3}{1.2.3} = 35$-highest number of ways!

- $C_4^7 = \dfrac{7.6.5.4}{1.2.3.4} = 35$-highest number of ways!

- $C_5^7 = \dfrac{7.6.5.4.3}{1.2.3.4.5} = 21$

- $C_6^7 = \dfrac{7.6.5.4.3.2}{1.2.3.4.5.6} = 7$

- $C_7^7 = \dfrac{7.6.5.4.3.2.1}{1.2.3.4.5.6.7} = 1$

Statement 1 is not sufficient to answer the question.

The correct answer would be among B, C, and E.

From statement 2:

The meaning of statement 1: *The number of generals in the team is such that if we increase the count of generals by one, it makes it possible to form teams with the highest number of ways.* is that r is such that the value of C_{r+1}^7 is the highest.

Leveraging from the analysis done in statement 1, we see that two values of r qualify: $r = 2$ or 3.

For $r = 2$, $C_3^7 = 35$-highest

Similarly, for $r = 3$, $C_4^7 = 35$-highest

Thus, $r = 2$ or 3–no unique value

Statement 2 is not sufficient to answer the question.

The correct answer would be between C and E.

Thus, from both the statements together:

By combining both the statements, we get $r = 3$–unique value.

The correct answer is option C.

Chapter 6

Probability

What are the chances of Messi winning the toss in a FIFA world
cup match? Well, ideally it's 50%! He has an equal chance of
winning and losing the toss, provided the coin and the trial are
fair.

It is very important that the coin tossed is fair, else the coin will be
called a biased coin, the outcomes of 'Head and Tail' would be influ-
enced, and the chances of getting a Head and getting a Tail will not be
50-50.

What do we mean when we say that the chance of getting a Head is 50%?

It means that if we toss a coin many number of times, say 100 times, it is likely that the
fair coin will fall Head 50 times and fall Tail 50 times. But can this occur practically?
The answer is no. Just to share a fact that Carolina Panthers has lost 13 tosses consec-
utively; however it is so rare that it happens in 1 out of 8192 cases!

So, is there a significance of 50-50? Yes, there is. If, say, the experiment of throwing a
fair coin is done over 100,000 times (Read: very large number of trials), it is very likely
that you get Head close to 50,000 times.

6.1   Chance vs. Probability

Chance is a term used by common people; it is measured on a scale of '100'. The count
of any event to occur out of 100 possibilities is a chance percent.

Probability is a term used by mathematicians; which is measured on a scale of '1' instead of '100'.

6.2   A few definitions

6.2.1   Experiment

Tossing a coin or throwing a die is an experiment. It is an activity that can be repeated
infinite number of times and produces a well-defined set of outcomes. In an experiment, only one of all the possible outcomes is the result. Repetition of an experiment
is called a **Trial**.

6.2.2   Event

In an experiment, getting a Head upon tossing a coin or getting a '3' on the upper
face upon throwing a die is an event. Events are a set of all possible outcomes of an
experiment. We may also talk about a favorable or an unfavorable event. Tossing a coin
renders two events: {Head and Tail}, while throwing a die renders six events: {1, 2, 3, 4,

5, 6}. In an experiment with a die, if you were to have '5' as an outcome, then getting a '5' is a favorable event, and not getting a '5' are unfavorable events.

6.2.3   Equally likely events

If the chances of occurrence of some events are equal, they are called equally likely events. For a fair die, the chance of the occurrence of '3' equals that of '5'. So, these events are equally likely. Similarly, for a coin, the chance of getting a 'Head' equals that of a 'Tail'.

6.2.4   Sample set

A set of all possible outcomes of an experiment is called the sample set. For a fair die, the sample set is {1, 2, 3, 4, 5, 6}; whereas for a coin, the sample set is {Head, Tail}.

$$\text{Probability of an event} = \frac{\text{Number of favorable events}}{\text{Total number of events}}$$

Question: What is the probability of getting an outcome as Head in an experiment of tossing a fair coin?

The sample set is {Head, Tail}, so only two events are possible; out of these two events, only one event—Head is the favorable event.

$$\text{P(Head)} = \frac{\text{Number of favorable events}}{\text{Total number of events}} = \frac{n(\text{favorable events})}{n(\text{total events})} = \frac{1}{2}$$

Question: In an experiment of throwing a die, what is the probability of getting an outcome as '2' or '4' on the upper face of an unbiased die?

The sample set is {1, 2, 3, 4, 5, 6}, so there are a total six events; out of these six events, two events: {2, 4} are the favorable events.

$$\text{Probability of '2' or '4'} = \frac{n(\text{favorable events})}{n(\text{total events})} = \frac{n\{2,4\}}{n\{1,2,3,4,5,6\}} = \frac{2}{6} = \frac{1}{3}$$

Sum of probabilities of all events = '1'. Event with probability = 1 is a **Certain event.**

$$\text{P(H or T)} = \frac{n(\text{favorable events})}{n(\text{total events})} = \frac{2}{2} = 1$$

Probability cannot be less than '0'. Event with probability = 0 is an **Impossible event.**

Probability (neither Head nor Tail) = $\dfrac{n(\text{favorable events})}{n(\text{total events})} = \dfrac{0}{2} = 0$

So, we can deduce that:

$$\boxed{0 \le P(A) \le 1}$$

Question: There are 2 red, 4 green, and 5 black balls in a bag. If a ball is drawn randomly, what is the probability that it is a green color ball?

$$P(G) = \dfrac{n(\text{ favorable events})}{n(\text{total events})} = \dfrac{4}{(2+4+5)} = \dfrac{4}{11}$$

6.3   An experiment with two dice

 **Die** is singular and **Dice** is plural. Two dice will have $6 \times 6 = 36$ sample points or possible events. The sample set of SUM would be $\{2, 3, 4, 5, 6, 7, 8, 9, 10, 11, 12\}$; each element in the set is the sum of outcomes on the upper face of each die.

Let us list down the number ways each sum can be formed.

Sum	Ways	Number of ways	Frequency distribution & Probabilities
2	{1,1}	1	$p = \dfrac{1}{36}$
3	{2,1}, {1,2}	2	$p = \dfrac{1}{18}$
4	{3,1}, {2,2}, {1,3}	3	$p = \dfrac{1}{12}$
5	{4,1}, {3,2}, {2,3}, {1,4}	4	$p = \dfrac{1}{9}$
6	{5,1}, {4,2}, {3,3}, {2,4}, {1,5}	5	$p = \dfrac{5}{36}$
7	{6,1}, {5,2}, {4,3}, {3,4}, {2,5}, {1,6}	6	$p = \dfrac{1}{6}$
8	{6,2}, {5,3}, {4,4}, {3,5}, {2,6}	5	$p = \dfrac{5}{36}$
9	{6,3}, {5,4}, {4,5}, {3,6}	4	$p = \dfrac{1}{9}$
10	{6,4}, {5,5}, {4,6}	3	$p = \dfrac{1}{12}$
11	{6,5}, {5,6}	2	$p = \dfrac{1}{18}$
12	{6,6}	1	$p = \dfrac{1}{36}$
	Total number of ways	36	

Memorise...

   1. If Sum ≤ 7, then Number of ways = Sum – 1

   2. If Sum ≥ 8, then Number of ways = 13 – Sum

Question: What is the probability of getting a sum of '5' on the upper faces of two unbiased dice?

The sample set is $\{2, 3, 4, 5, 6, 7, 8, 9, 10, 11, 12\}$; and there are a total 36 possible events.

$$\text{Probability of getting a sum of '5'} = \frac{n(\text{favorable events})}{n(\text{total events})} = \frac{4}{36} = \frac{1}{9}$$

6.4   A few more definitions

6.4.1   Mutually Exclusive Events

If two events cannot occur together, they are called **Mutually Exclusive** events or **Disjoint** events.

Example: Getting a Head and a Tail on the upper face of a coin; another example, getting a '3' and a '5' in a throw of a die.

Since for a coin, only one of the two events—Head or Tail will occur at a time, hence they are mutually exclusive events; similarly, if '3' appears on the upper face of the die, it is obvious that '5' will not appear.

Following Venn diagram represents the scenario.

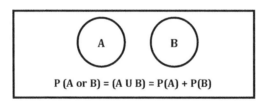

However, an event of getting '3' and 'prime number' in a throw of a die is not mutually exclusive as '3' is an element of the set of prime numbers.

If the events are joint or non-mutually exclusive, then the following formula applies.

P(A or B) = P(A ∪ B) = P(A) + P(B) – P(A & B)

Following Venn diagram represents the scenario.

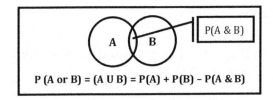

The table below depicts the difference between mutually exclusive and joint events with an application of an example.

Event	Example	Solution
Disjoint (Mutually exclusive)	A die is rolled. What is the probability of getting a '3' or a '5' on the upper face of the die?	P('3') = 1/6; P('5') = 1/6; So, P('3' or '5') = (1/6) + (1/6) = 1/3.
Joint	A die is rolled. What is the probability of getting a '3' or a 'Prime number' on the upper face of the die?	P('3') = 1/6; P('Prime') = 3/6 = 1/2; P('3' & 'P') = 1/6 ('3' is common in Prime numbers: 2, 3, and 5); So, P('3' or 'P') = (1/6) + (1/2) − (1/6) = 1/2.

6.4.2 Independent Events

Two events are called independent if the occurrence of one event does not affect the occurrence of the other.

Example: In a throw of two dice, the occurrence of a '3' on the first die does not influence the occurrence of any number on the second die; hence these events are independent events.

For independent events, **P(A & B) = P(A ∩ B) = P(A) × P(B)**

If the events are not independent, then the concept of 'conditional probability' is involved; however this concept is not frequently tested on the GMAT.

6.4.3 Exhaustive event

A set of events is called **Exhaustive** if there is no possibility of any other event to occur other than the events in the set; in other words, one of those events must occur. For example: In the toss of a coin, Events of a Head and a Tail are exhaustive events. (assuming, of course, that the coin does not land on its side!)

6.5   AND vs. OR rule

In a nut shell, you must know rules for probability calculations on the GMAT: "AND" means MULTIPLY, and "OR" means ADDITION.

Concept	Application	Example	Solution
AND	×; multiply the probabilities	A coin is tossed twice. What is the probability of getting a Head in first trial, and Tail in the second trial?	P(Head in I trial) = 1/2; P(Tail in II trial) = 1/2; So, P(HT) = (1/2) × (1/2) = 1/4.
OR	+; add the probabilities	A die is rolled. What is the probability of getting a '3' **or** an 'Even number' on the upper face of the die?	P('3') = 1/6; P('E') = 3/6 = 1/2; So, P('3' or 'E') = (1/6) + (1/2) = 2/3.

6.6   Conditional Probability

The concept of conditional probability relates to deducing the probability of an event given that another event has already occurred. This concept is important since the occurrence of one event can affect the probability of a dependent event.

The conditional probability of A given B is denoted by $P(A|B)$, it means probability of A if event B has occurred.

$$P(A|B) = \frac{P(A \cap B)}{P(B)}$$

Question: What is the probability of getting a '3' on the upper face of a die given that the number appeared is a 'Prime number'?

Say, P('3') = probability of getting a '3';
and P('P') = probability of getting a 'Prime number'

We know that P('P') = 1/2;
and P('3'∩'P') = 1/6

So, $P(3|P) = \dfrac{P(3 \cap P)}{P(P)} = \dfrac{1/6}{1/2} = 1/3$

Logical deduction approach:

Since there are only three prime numbers: 2, 3, & 5 and '3' is one of them, hence the chance of getting '3' out of '2', '3' and '5' is 33.33% = 1/3.

6.7 Independent and Dependent Events

- For **Independent Events: P(A|B) = P(A)**;

- For **Dependent Events: P(A|B) ≠ P(A)**

Question: A bag contains 3 yellow and 7 blue marbles. What is the probability of drawing a yellow marble in the first draw and then drawing a blue marble in the second draw?

Let us understand the concept of dependent event.

The second event–drawing a blue marble–is a dependent event since the draw of a yellow marble in the first draw will increase the probability of drawing a blue marble in the second draw; while the draw of a blue marble in the first draw will decrease the probability of drawing another blue marble in the second draw. So the second event is a dependent event.

Let us see how.

(1) If a yellow marble is drawn in the first draw, then the bag will contain $\cancel{3}2$ yellow and 7 blue marbles; this makes the probability of drawing the blue marble in the second draw equals to 7/(2 + 7) = 7/9.

(2) If a blue marble is drawn in the first draw, then the bag will contain 3 yellow and $\cancel{7}6$ blue marbles; this makes the probability of drawing the blue marble in the second draw equals to 6/(3 + 6) = 6/9 = 2/3.

Clearly, 7/9 ≠ 2/3 implies that the probability of the second event is dependent on that of the first event.

Coming back to the question...

Drawing a yellow marble in the first draw = 3/10.
Drawing a blue marble in the second draw = 7/9.

So, the probability of drawing a yellow marble in the first draw, and blue marble in the second draw = (3/10) × (7/9) = 7/30.

6.8   Complement of an Event

If the occurrence of an event is denoted as A, then its non-occurrence is denoted as A' or A^C.

=> **Probability of occurrence an event + Probability of non-occurrence an event = 1.**

So, $P(A')$ or $P(A^C) = 1 - P(A)$;

or $P(A) + P(A') = 1$

Question: If a coin is tossed 3 times, what is the probability that it lands up on heads at least once?

Traditional approach:

P (Head ≥ 1) = P (Head = 1; Tail = 2) + P (Head = 2; Tail = 1) + P (Head = 3; Tail = none);

=> (Head = 1; Tail = 2) can occur in 3 ways; HTT, THT, and TTH;

For each way, P (Head = 1; Tail = 2) = (1/2) × (1/2 × 1/2) = 1/8;

So, for all 3 ways, P (Head = 1; Tail = 2) = 3 × (1/8) = 3/8.

=> Similarly, (Head = 2; Tail = 1) can occur in 3 ways; HHT, THH, and HTH;

Again, for each way, P (Head = 2; Tail = 1) = (1/2) × (1/2 × 1/2) = 1/8;

So, for all 3 ways, P (Head = 2; Tail = 1) = 3 × (1/8) = 3/8.

=> At last, (Head = 3; Tail = none) can occur in only one way; HHH;

P (Head = 3; Tail = none) = (1/2 × 1/2 × 1/2) = 1/8.

So, P (Head ≥ 1) = P (Head = 1; Tail = 2) + P (Head = 2; Tail = 1) + P (Head = 3; Tail = none);
                  = 3/8 + 3/8 + 1/8
                  = 7/8.

This approach is time consuming. Let us see an alternate approach.

Alternate approach:

P (Head ≥ 1) = 1 − P (Head < 1)′ = 1 − P (Head = 0; Tail = 3)

$$= 1 − (1/2 \times 1/2 \times 1/2)$$

$$= 7/8.$$

So, the learning is that we can make use of the concept of complement of an event to shorten the calculations.

6.9 Application of combination

What if the question is like the following?

Question: If a coin is tossed 3 times, what is the probability that it lands up on Head at least twice?

In this question, the alternate approach and the traditional approach will take almost the same time.

Alternate approach:

P (Head ≥ 2) = 1 − P (Head < 2)′ = 1 − P (Head = 0; Tail = 3) − P (Head = 1; Tail = 2)

You will have to do the calculations twice–once for P (Head = 0; Tail = 3), and then for P (Head = 1; Tail = 2).

Traditional approach:

P (Head ≥ 2) = P (Head = 2; Tail = 1) + P (Head = 3; Tail = none)

Again, you will have to do the calculations twice–once for P (Head = 2; Tail = 1), and then for P (Head = 3; Tail = none). Practically there is no saving of time!

However, with the application of the concept of combination, we can save some time.

Let us take a seemingly time-consuming question.

Question: If a coin is tossed 5 times, what is the probability that it lands up on Head at least thrice?

P (Head ≥ 3) = P (Head = 3; Tail = 2) + P (Head = 4; Tail = 1) + P (Head = 5; Tail = none)

The meaning of (Head = 3; Tail = 2) is that we want 3 Heads occurring in 3 out of 5 trials, so it can be deduced that we want to choose 3 events out of 5 events, which is equal to C_3^5.

So, P (Head = 3; Tail = 2) = $C_3^5 \times [(1/2 \times 1/2 \times 1/2) \times (1/2 \times 1/2)]$
= $C_2^5 \times (1/2)^5$ = (5.4)/(1.2) × $(1/2)^5$ = (5.4)/(1.2) × $(1/2)^5$ = $5/2^4$.
(Note that $C_3^5 = C_2^5$)

Similarly, P (Head = 4; Tail = 1) = $C_4^5 \times [(1/2 \times 1/2 \times 1/2 \times 1/2) \times (1/2)]$
= $C_1^5 \times (1/2)^5$ = $5/2^5$.

And, P (Head = 5; Tail = none) = $C_5^5 \times (1/2 \times 1/2 \times 1/2 \times 1/2 \times 1/2)$ = $1 \times (1/2)^5$ = 2^5.

So, P (Head ≥ 3) = $5/2^4 + 5/2^5 + 1/2^5$ = $16/2^5$ = 1/2.

P (Head ≥ 3) = 1/2.

Let us see one more question.

Question: A bag contains 4 yellow and 5 blue marbles. If three marbles are drawn simultaneously, what is the probability of drawing a yellow and two blue marbles?

P(Y = 1; B = 2)

$$= \frac{(\text{\# of ways one yellow marble can be drawn}) \times (\text{\# of ways two blue marbles can be drawn})}{(\text{\# of ways three marbles can be drawn})}$$

$$= \frac{(C_1^4).(C_2^5)}{C_3^9} = 4 \times \left[\frac{\frac{5.4}{1.2}}{\frac{9.8.7}{1.2.3}} \right] = \frac{10}{21}.$$

Now we see exam-like questions in the next chapter.

Chapter 7

Practice Questions

7.1 Problem Solving

1. A box contains 30 balls, of which 10 are black, 10 are green, and 10 are yellow. If two balls are drawn from the box at random, what is the probability that both the balls will be green?

   (A) 3/29

   (B) 1/9

   (C) 1/3

   (D) 2/3

   (E) 1

   Solve yourself:

2. An unbiased coin is tossed thrice. What is the probability of getting at least one Head?

   (A) 1/8

   (B) 3/8

   (C) 1/2

   (D) 7/8

   (E) 1

   Solve yourself:

3. A class of 36 students has an equal number of boys and girls. Four students are randomly selected to form a cultural committee. If the first three selected students are boys, what is the probability that the 4ᵗʰ student is also a boy?

   (A) 1/33

   (B) 1/15

   (C) 5/12

   (D) 5/11

(E) 12/13

Solve yourself:

4. A delegation of 9 diplomats comprises 3 Japanese and 6 Chinese. If 3 diplomats are to be chosen at random from the delegation, what is the probability that at least 2 diplomats are Japanese?

   (A) 1/12
   (B) 3/14
   (C) 19/84
   (D) 1/3
   (E) 1/2

   Solve yourself:

5. John, Peter, and Harry are given an assignment to collectively solve a problem. The probabilities of John, Peter and Harry to solve the problem individually are 4/5, 2/3, and 3/4 respectively. What is the probability that the problem will not be solved?

   (A) 1/60
   (B) 13/60
   (C) 2/3
   (D) 47/60
   (E) 59/60

   Solve yourself:

6. John and Harry are among the 5 promising soccer players in the school. 3 out of 5 players are to be chosen at random. What is the probability that both John and Harry would be chosen?

  (A) 1/10

  (B) 1/5

  (C) 3/10

  (D) 2/5

  (E) 3/5

  Solve yourself:

7. Three actors are to be chosen out of five — Jack, Steve, Elad, Suzy, and Ali. What is the probability that Jack and Steve would be chosen, but Suzy would be left out?

  (A) 1/5

  (B) 2/5

  (C) 3/5

  (D) 7/10

  (E) 9/10

  Solve yourself:

8. A box contains p number of silver coins and q number of gold coins. One coin is randomly drawn from the box but not replaced; thereafter a second coin is randomly drawn. What is the probability that the first coin drawn is silver and the second is gold?

  (A) $\left(\dfrac{p}{p+q}\right)\left(\dfrac{q}{p+q}\right)$

  (B) $\left(\dfrac{p}{p+q}\right)\left(\dfrac{p-1}{p+q-1}\right)$

(C) $\left(\dfrac{pq}{p+q}\right)$

(D) $\left(\dfrac{p-1}{p+q}\right)\left(\dfrac{q-1}{p+q}\right)$

(E) $\left(\dfrac{p}{p+q}\right)\left(\dfrac{q}{p+q-1}\right)$

Solve yourself:

9. A super mall issues coupons to its customers at the entrance of the mall. The coupons are numbered from 100 to 400, inclusive. Customers who have coupons with the numbers divisible by '2' will win gifts. What is the probability that a random customer wins a gift?

(A) 149/300

(B) 150/301

(C) 151/301

(D) 1/2

(E) 151/300

Solve yourself:

10. There are 2 groups — Group A comprises of only 50 married men, while group B comprises of only 40 married women. Between these groups, there are only 5 husband-wife pairs. If one man and one woman is randomly chosen from each group, what is the probability that they make a husband-wife pair?

(A) 1/400

(B) 1/80

(C) 1/18

(D) 1/9

(E) 9/40

Solve yourself:

11. A box contains 30 balls, of which 10 are black, 10 are green, and 10 are yellow balls. If two balls are drawn from the box at random one after the other (with replacement), what is the probability that both the balls will be green?

   (A) 3/29
   (B) 1/9
   (C) 1/4
   (D) 1/3
   (E) 2/3

   Solve yourself:

12. A box contains 4 black and few green balls. If two balls are drawn from the box at random, and the probability that both the balls are black is 1/6, how many green balls are in the box?

   (A) 3
   (B) 4
   (C) 5
   (D) 6
   (E) 9

   Solve yourself:

13. In the GMAT—Quantitative Ability section, there are 41 questions with 5 options. A candidate knows the correct answers of 16 questions, unsure between 2 options for 10 questions, unsure among 3 options for 6 questions, unsure among 4 options for 4 questions, and unsure among all 5 options for 5 questions. How many questions can he probably mark correct?

(A) 24

(B) 25

(C) 26

(D) 27

(E) 28

Solve yourself:

14. A tool-box contains 10 spanners, out of which 3 are defective. If a mechanic randomly selects 2 spanners at a time, what is the probability that at least one spanner will be defective?

(A) 2/9

(B) 3/10

(C) 7/15

(D) 8/15

(E) 14/15

Solve yourself:

15. A class comprises of 20 students, out of which 15 are boys and the rest are girls. If a committee of 3 students is to be formed, what is the probability that there would be only one boy in the committee?

(A) 5/38

(B) 3/10

(C) 35/76

(D) 41/76

(E) 7/10

Solve yourself:

16. The probability that a man can shoot and hit a target is 1/100. If the man fires 100 rounds, what is the probability that all the 100 shots do not miss the target?

(A) $\left(\dfrac{1}{10}\right)^{200}$

(B) $\dfrac{10^{200} - 1}{10^{200}}$

(C) $\left(\dfrac{1}{100}\right)^{2}$

(D) $\left(\dfrac{99}{100}\right)^{100}$

(E) $\dfrac{(100^{100} - 99^{100})}{100^{100}}$

Solve yourself:

17. A group of 12 people comprises 3 Japanese, 4 Australians, and 5 Chinese. If 4 people are to be chosen at random from the group to form a committee, what is the probability that 2 members are Japanese?

(A) 3/55

(B) 12/55

(C) 3/11

(D) 49/55

(E) 10/11

Solve yourself:

18. A gambler bets everyday on soccer games. If the probability of him loosing the bet each day is 0.4, what is the probability that he wins on only 2 days out of 3 days he bets?

   (A) 0.096

   (B) 0.144

   (C) 0.16

   (D) 0.36

   (E) 0.432

   Solve yourself:

19. Four friends A, B, C and D stand in a line for a photograph. What is the probability that A stands to the immediate left of C?

   (A) $\dfrac{1}{6}$

   (B) $\dfrac{1}{4}$

   (C) $\dfrac{1}{3}$

   (D) $\dfrac{1}{2}$

   (E) 1

   Solve yourself:

20. A bag has 20 blue and 10 red balls. What is the probability of drawing two balls simultaneously so that they are not of the same color?

    (A) 0.13

    (B) 0.26

    (C) 0.36

    (D) 0.46

    (E) 1

Solve yourself:

21. Probability that a missile will hit its target is 0.6. If three missiles are fired at the target, what is the probability of hitting the target at least once?

    (A) 0.096

    (B) 0.6

    (C) 0.936

    (D) 0.964

    (E) 1

Solve yourself:

22. What is the probability of randomly selecting two numbers simultaneously from numbers 1 to 100 (both inclusive) so that the two numbers are odd perfect squares?

    (A) $\dfrac{1}{990}$

    (B) $\dfrac{1}{495}$

    (C) $\dfrac{1}{20}$

    (D) $\dfrac{1}{10}$

(E) $\dfrac{1}{5}$

Solve yourself:

23. What is the probability of randomly selecting two numbers simultaneously from numbers 1 to 50 (both inclusive) so that the two numbers are neither prime nor perfect squares?

(A) 0.50

(B) 0.40

(C) 0.31

(D) 0.21

(E) 0.11

Solve yourself:

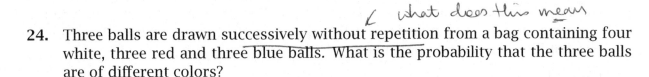

24. Three balls are drawn successively without repetition from a bag containing four white, three red and three blue balls. What is the probability that the three balls are of different colors?

(A) $\dfrac{1}{20}$

(B) $\dfrac{1}{5}$

(C) $\dfrac{2}{9}$

(D) $\dfrac{5}{21}$

(E) $\dfrac{3}{10}$

Solve yourself:

25. There are two bags, one contains three white and two black balls, while the other contains four white and five black balls. What is the probability that if one ball is drawn from each bag, they will be of the same color?

(A) $\dfrac{11}{45}$

(B) $\dfrac{22}{45}$

(C) $\dfrac{1}{2}$

(D) $\dfrac{3}{4}$

(E) 1

Solve yourself:

26. A box contains three blue and two red balls, while another box contains four green and two white balls. A coin is tossed. If 'heads' appears, a ball is drawn from the first box and if a tail appears, a ball is drawn from the second box. What is the probability of drawing a blue ball?

(A) 0.1

(B) 0.2

(C) 0.3

(D) 0.6

(E) 0.7

Solve yourself:

27. If for a biased die, the probability of appearance of an even number is double that of an odd number, what is the probability of consecutive 6s appearing on two throws of the die?

(A) $\dfrac{1}{36}$

(B) $\dfrac{2}{9}$

(C) $\dfrac{4}{81}$

(D) $\dfrac{5}{81}$

(E) $\dfrac{7}{81}$

Solve yourself:

28. Three balls are simultaneously drawn from a box containing five yellow and four green balls. What is the probability that the three balls are not all of the same color?

(A) 0.167

(B) 0.33

(C) 0.83

(D) 0.89

(E) 1

Solve yourself:

29. Given that

- A = Probability of drawing two red balls from a bag containing 12 red and 10 blue balls

- B = Probability of drawing two blue balls from a bag containing 12 red and 10 blue balls

- C = Probability of drawing one red and one blue ball from a bag containing 12 red and 10 blue balls

Which of the following statement is correct?

(A) $A < B < C$

(B) $A > C > B$

(C) $A > B > C$

(D) $C > A > B$

(E) $A < C < B$

Solve yourself:

30. Given that

- A = Probability of getting all heads when three coins are tossed

- B = Probability of getting all tails when three coins are tossed

- C = Probability of getting two heads and one tail when three coins are tossed

Which of the following statement is correct?

(A) $A = 3B = 6C$

(B) $A = C = 3B$

(C) $A = B = C$

(D) $C = 3A = 3B$

(E) $3C = A = B$

Solve yourself:

31. What is the probability of selecting x from the set $\{-2, 0, 2, 4, 6\}$ such that $x^2 \leq$ 16?

(A) $\dfrac{1}{5}$

(B) $\dfrac{2}{5}$

(C) $\dfrac{3}{5}$

(D) $\dfrac{4}{5}$

(E) $\dfrac{5}{6}$

Solve yourself:

32. What is the probability of obtaining the same number on each throw if a die is thrown thrice?

(A) $\dfrac{1}{36}$

(B) $\dfrac{1}{3}$

(C) $\dfrac{1}{2}$

(D) $\dfrac{2}{3}$

(E) $\dfrac{5}{6}$

Solve yourself:

33. What is the probability of obtaining an odd number or a prime number on one throw of a dice?

(A) $\dfrac{1}{6}$

(B) $\dfrac{1}{3}$

(C) $\dfrac{2}{3}$

(D) $\dfrac{3}{4}$

(E) $\dfrac{5}{6}$

Solve yourself:

34. What is the probability of getting a number on the first throw greater than that on the second throw when a dice is thrown twice?

(A) $\dfrac{1}{6}$

(B) $\dfrac{5}{12}$

(C) $\dfrac{7}{12}$

(D) $\dfrac{2}{3}$

(E) $\dfrac{5}{6}$

Solve yourself:

35. What is the probability of selecting two cards successively with replacement from five cards numbered '1' to '5' so that the sum of the numbers is '8'?

(A) $\dfrac{3}{25}$

(B) $\dfrac{2}{5}$

(C) $\dfrac{3}{5}$

(D) $\dfrac{4}{5}$

(E) $\dfrac{5}{7}$

Solve yourself:

36. What is the probability of obtaining '3' at least once on throwing a dice twice?

   (A) $\dfrac{1}{9}$

   (B) $\dfrac{5}{18}$

   (C) $\dfrac{11}{36}$

   (D) $\dfrac{7}{18}$

   (E) $\dfrac{25}{36}$

   Solve yourself:

37. What is the probability of choosing a number from the set such that the selected number is the mean of the set: {1, 2, 2, 3, 4, 5, 5, 5, 9}?

   (A) $\dfrac{1}{12}$

   (B) $\dfrac{1}{10}$

   (C) $\dfrac{1}{9}$

   (D) $\dfrac{1}{8}$

   (E) $\dfrac{2}{9}$

Solve yourself:

38. What is the probability of selecting two numbers, one from set A: {1, 3, 6} and the other from B: {2, 3, 8} so that the sum of the numbers is 9?

(A) $\dfrac{1}{2}$

(B) $\dfrac{2}{9}$

(C) $\dfrac{1}{9}$

(D) $\dfrac{1}{10}$

(E) $\dfrac{1}{12}$

Solve yourself:

39. What is the probability of selecting two numbers, one from set A: {1, 3, 6} and the other from B: {2, 3, 8} so that the product of the numbers is 9?

(A) $\dfrac{1}{2}$

(B) $\dfrac{2}{9}$

(C) $\dfrac{1}{9}$

(D) $\dfrac{1}{10}$

(E) $\dfrac{1}{12}$

Solve yourself:

40. How many red balls are there in a bag that contains 24 balls of red, blue and green colors; given that the probability of drawing a blue ball is $\frac{1}{4}$ and the probability of drawing a green ball is $\frac{2}{3}$?

    (A) One

    (B) Two

    (C) Three

    (D) Four

    (E) Five

Solve yourself:

41.

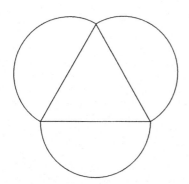

Above figure shows a designer dartboard. It has a triangle at the center with side 4 cm. Each side of the triangle is the diameter of respective semi-circle. If Brian throws a dart, and it hits the dartboard, what is the probability that it hits triangular part of the dartboard?

    (A) 1/4

    (B) 1/2

    (C) $\dfrac{2\sqrt{3}}{2\sqrt{3} + 6\pi}$

(D) $\dfrac{4\sqrt{3}}{4\sqrt{3}+6\pi}$

(E) $\dfrac{3\sqrt{3}}{4\sqrt{3}+6\pi}$

Solve yourself:

42. A box contains 5 black and some green balls. If two balls are drawn from the box at random, and the probability that both the balls are green is 1/6, how many green balls are in the box?

(A) 3

(B) 4

(C) 5

(D) 6

(E) 8

Solve yourself:

43.

Above figure shows a dartboard. Radius of the the outermost circle is 4 cm., the radius of the innermost black circle is 1 cm., and the width of the black ring is 1 cm. If Brian throws a dart, and it hits the dartboard, what is the probability that it hits any of the black parts of the dartboard?

(A) 1/8

(B) 1/4

(C) 3/8

(D) 1/2

(E) 5/8

Solve yourself:

7.2 Data Sufficiency

Data sufficiency questions have five standard options. They are listed below and will not be repeated for each question.

(A) Statement (1) ALONE is sufficient, but statement (2) ALONE is not sufficient to answer the question asked.

(B) Statement (2) ALONE is sufficient, but statement (1) ALONE is not sufficient to answer the question asked.

(C) both the statements (1) and (2) TOGETHER are sufficient to answer the question asked, but NEITHER statement ALONE is sufficient to answer the question asked.

(D) EACH statement ALONE is sufficient to answer the question asked.

(E) Statements (1) and (2) TOGETHER are NOT sufficient to answer the question asked, and additional data specific to the problem are needed.

44. There are 100 coins in a box. They are either gold, solver, or bronze; each of them is engraved with one of the 26 English alphabet. If one coin is selected at random from the box, what is the probability that the coin selected would be either a gold coin or a coin engraved with a vowel or both?

   (1) Probability that the selected coin would be a gold coin engraved with vowel is 0.2.

   (2) Sum of the probability of randomly selecting a gold coin and the probability of randomly selecting a coin engraved with vowel is 0.4.

   Solve yourself:

45. City college of Liberal arts conducts language courses for French, Spanish, and German. A student can choose one or more languages to study. Is the probability of selecting a random student who studies French and Spanish equal to 0.2?

   (1) Probability that a randomly selected student studies French is 0.8.

   (2) Probability that a randomly selected student studies Spanish is 0.4.

   Solve yourself:

46. Following question is a modified version of the previous question. Read the question stem carefully.

   Is the probability of selecting a random student who studies French and Spanish equals 0.1?

   (1) Probability that a randomly selected student studies French is 0.8.

   (2) Probability that a randomly selected student studies Spanish is 0.4.

   Solve yourself:

47. A person bets in a game. There are x number of identical black balls, y number of identical white balls, and z number of identical green balls in a box. He has to draw a black ball from the box to win the bet. Is the number of black balls less than the total number of white and green balls combined?

(1) Probability of drawing a green ball is double the probability of drawing a white ball.

(2) Probability of drawing a black ball is 1.5 times the probability of drawing a green ball.

Solve yourself:

48. In a hospital, there are 87 patients, out of which 69 are heart patients. If a patient is randomly selected, what is the probability that he or she is a heart patient as well as a smoker?

(1) There are 23 patients who smoke.

(2) 46 heart patients do not smoke.

Solve yourself:

49. A tool-box contains 10 spanners, out of which x are defective. If a mechanic randomly selects 2 spanners at a time, what is the value of x?

(1) Probability that both the selected spanners are defective is 2/15.

(2) Probability that no spanner is defective is 1/3.

Solve yourself:

50. A box contains 10 black, 10 green, and some yellow balls. If two balls are randomly drawn from the box, what is the probability that both the balls will be green?

   (1)   There are as many yellow balls as black and green balls combined.

   (2)   Probability of drawing a yellow ball is double the probability of drawing a black ball.

Solve yourself:

51. A box contains 10 balls of four colors. Is the probability of drawing a colored ball which are most in number in the box equals 4 times the probability of drawing a colored ball which are the least in number?

   (1)   No two color balls are equal in number.

   (2)   Probability of drawing any one color ball is NOT equal to the probability of drawing any other color ball.

Solve yourself:

52. John, Peter, and Harry are given an assignment to collectively solve a problem. What is the probability that the problem will not be solved?

   (1)   Sum of probabilities that any two of them can solve and the other cannot solve is 1/2.

   (2)   Sum of probabilities that any one of them can solve and the other two cannot solve is 1/3.

Solve yourself:

53. A team plays two matches. There are only three results possible: Win, Loss, and Draw. What is the probability that the team does not lose any of the matches?

  (1) Probability of losing a match is 1/3.

  (2) Sum of probability of winning a match and probability of losing a match is 2/3.

  Solve yourself:

54. *Following question is a modified version of the previous question.*

A team plays two matches. There are only three results possible: Win, Loss, and Draw. What is the probability that the team **loses at the most one** match?

  (1) Probability of losing a match is 1/3.

  (2) Sum of probability of winning a match and probability of losing a match is 2/3.

  Solve yourself:

55. If $x + y = 5$, is $P(x \geq 1) = 1$?

  (1) Both x and y are positive integers.

  (2) One of x and y is a non-negative integer, and the other is a positive integer less than 5.

  Solve yourself:

56. Twenty families live in a residential society. Each family has either 0, 1, 2, or 3 children.

If P(# of children = 2) = 1/4, then what is the value of P(# of children = 3)?

    (1)   P(# of children = none) + P(# of children = 1) = 3/10.

    (2) $\dfrac{\text{P(\# of children = none)}}{\text{P(\# of children = 3)}} = 1/3.$

Solve yourself:

57. If a set contains consecutive integers from 1 through n, both inclusive, what is the probability that a number randomly selected from the set is divisible by '3'?

    (1)   The probability that a number randomly selected from the set is divisible by '2' is 36/73.

    (2) $n < 200$.

Solve yourself:

58. If, in an urn, the ratio of number of red balls to number of yellow balls to number of green balls is $n : p : k$, then what is the probability that a ball chosen randomly from the urn is a green ball?

    (1)   The ratio of number of red balls to number of yellow balls in the urn is $47 : 37$.

    (2)   The ratio of number of yellow balls to number of green balls in the urn is $148 : 67$.

Solve yourself:

59. If in an urn, the ratio of number of red balls to number of yellow balls to number of green balls is $n : p : k$, then what is the probability that a ball chosen randomly from the urn is a green ball?

    (1)   The ratio of number of red balls to number of yellow balls in the urn is $2 : 3$.

    (2)   Total number of balls in the urn is 43.

Solve yourself:

60. An airplane has two engines, one on left and one on right. The failure or non-failure of each engine is independent of the other. If the airplane can fly with one engine, what is the probability that the airplane cannot fly at all?

    (1)   The probability that the left engine works is 4/7.

    (2)   The probability that the right engine works is 4/7.

Solve yourself:

61. A child has to select n numbers one by one from the numbers 1 to 15. What is the probability that the child selects the numbers in ascending order?

    (1)   The third number selected by the child is 8

    (2) $n = 5$

Solve yourself:

62. A biased coin (a coin that does not have equal chances of occurrence of ''Head' and 'Tail') is tossed twice. What is the ratio of probability of getting 'Head' on a single toss to probability of getting 'Tail' on a single toss?

    (1)   The probability of getting at least one 'Head' on two tosses is 5/9.

    (2)   The probability of getting at least one 'Tail' on two tosses is 8/9.

    Solve yourself:

63. If there are two red, four green, and at least one black ball, are there balls of two different colors in equal number?

    (1)   The probability of drawing a green ball lies between 2/5 and 1/2, inclusive.

    (2)   The probability of drawing a black ball lies between 2/5 and 1/2, inclusive.

    Solve yourself:

64. A box has few red, few green and few black balls. Are red balls the most in number in the box?

    (1)   The ratio of drawing two red balls to the probability of drawing a green ball and a black ball is $\dfrac{1}{12}$.

    (2)   The ratio of drawing two green balls to the probability of drawing a red ball and a black ball is $\dfrac{3}{8}$.

    Solve yourself:

65. Three students make a team. What is the probability that the team solve a problem?

    (1)   The probability that at least one of them can solve the problem is 1/3.

    (2)   The probability that none can solve the problem is 2/3.

Solve yourself:

Chapter 8

Answer Key

8.1 Problem Solving

(1) A

(2) D

(3) D

(4) C

(5) A

(6) C

(7) A

(8) E

(9) C

(10) A

(11) B

(12) C

(13) B

(14) D

(15) A

(16) E

(17) B

(18) E

(19) B

(20) D

(21) C

(22) B

(23) C

(24) E

(25) B

(26) C

(27) C

(28) C

(29) D

(30) D

(31) A

(32) A

(33) C

(34) B

(35) A

(36) C

(37) C

(38) B

(39) C

(40) B

(41) D

(42) B

(43) C

8.2 Data Sufficiency

(44) C	(52) A	(60) C
(45) E	(53) A	(61) B
(46) C	(54) A	(62) D
(47) C	(55) D	(63) C
(48) B	(56) A	(64) C
(49) D	(57) C	(65) D
(50) D	(58) C	
(51) E	(59) C	

Chapter 9

Solutions

9.1 Problem Solving

1. Probability of an event = $\dfrac{\text{Number of favorable events}}{\text{Number of total events}}$;

    Here, number of favorable events = number of ways 2 green balls can be selected from 10 balls = C_2^{10};

    Number of total events = number of ways 2 balls can be selected from 30 balls = C_2^{30}

    Hence, probability of getting both the green balls = $\dfrac{C_2^{10}}{C_2^{30}} = \dfrac{10.9/1.2}{30.29/1.2} = \dfrac{3}{29}$

    The correct answer is option A.

2. Since the coin is unbiased, it means that probabilities of getting a 'Head' or getting a 'Tail' upon a single toss are equal = 1/2.

    Traditional approach of solving this question would be to find the probability for each time the coin turns Head and then add them, but that is a lengthy process.

    An efficient approach would be to find out the probability of not getting Head EVEN once, and then deducting it from total probability (1); this will assure that we get the Heads—one time, two times, and all three times.

    So, probability of getting at least one Head

    = 1 - (Probability of getting Tails in all 3 tosses)

    $= 1 - \left(\dfrac{1}{2}\cdot\dfrac{1}{2}\cdot\dfrac{1}{2}\right) = 1 - \dfrac{1}{8} = \dfrac{7}{8}$.

    The correct answer is option D.

3. Number of students = 36; Number of Boys = 18, so, number of girls = 18.

    Since the 3 selected students are boys, the number of boys remaining = 15. & total number of students remaining = 33.

    So, the probability of selecting 4th boy

    $= \dfrac{\text{Number of Boys remaining}}{\text{Total no. of students remaining}} = 15/33 = 5/11.$

The correct answer is option D.

Remember that this question is different from a similar question: ...*what is the probability that all the students selected are boys?* The difference is that in this question, 4 boys and no girl are to be chosen, while in the earlier one, 3 boys were already chosen, and only the 4th boy was to be chosen.

We will deal with this kind of question in subsequent questions.

4. Number of diplomats = 9; Number of Japanese = 3; & Number of Chinese = 6.

    The probability of choosing at least 2 Japanese

    = P (Japanese = 2, Chinese = 1) + P (Japanese = 3, Chinese = none)

    $\Rightarrow$ P (Japanese = 2, Chinese = 1) = $\dfrac{C_2^3 . C_1^6}{C_3^9} = \dfrac{C_1^3 . C_1^6}{C_3^9} = \dfrac{3.6}{\dfrac{9.8.7}{1.2.3}} = 3/14; [C_r^n = C_{n-r}^n]$

    $\Rightarrow$ P (Japanese = 3, Chinese = none) = $\dfrac{C_3^3}{C_3^9} = \dfrac{1}{\dfrac{9.8.7}{1.2.3}} = 1/84; [C_n^n = 1]$

    Hence, the probability of choosing at least 2 Japanese = 3/14 + 1/84 = 19/84

    The correct answer is option C.

5. The problem will not be solved in only condition when none among John, Peter, and Harry is able to solve it. Even if one of them could crack it, the problem will be solved as they have to solve it collectively.

    So, probability of not solving the problem = P(John could not solve it) × P(Peter could not solve it) × P(Harry could not solve it)

    $\Rightarrow \left(1 - \dfrac{4}{5}\right) . \left(1 - \dfrac{2}{3}\right) . \left(1 - \dfrac{3}{4}\right) = \dfrac{1}{5} . \dfrac{1}{3} . \dfrac{1}{4} = \dfrac{1}{60}$

    The correct answer is option A.

6. Total number of players = 5;

    Number of players apart from John and Harry = 3;

    Probability of choosing both John and Harry (2 players) only one among the rest

$$= \frac{C_2^2 . C_1^3}{C_3^5} = \frac{1.3}{\frac{5.4.3}{1.2.3}} = 3/10.$$

The correct answer is option C.

7. Total Number of actors = 5;

    Since Jack and Steve need to be in the selection and Suzy is to be left out, only one selection matters.

    Number of actors apart from Jack, Steve, and Suzy = 2;

    Probability of choosing 3 actors, incl. Jack and Steve, but not Suzy = $\dfrac{C_1^2}{C_3^5}$ = 1/5

    The correct answer is option A.

8. Number of silver coins = p; Number of gold coins = q;
    so total umber of coins = $p + q$;

    The probability of getting 1st coin a silver and 2nd coin a gold
    = P (silver coin) $\times$ P (gold coin)

    $\Rightarrow$ P (silver coin) = $\dfrac{C_1^p}{C_1^{p+q}} = \dfrac{p}{p+q}$

    After 1st draw, there would be only $p + q - 1$ number of coins left.

    $\Rightarrow$ So, P (gold coin) = $\dfrac{C_1^q}{C_1^{p+q-1}} = \dfrac{q}{p+q-1}$

    $\Rightarrow$ Hence, the probability of getting 1st coin a silver and 2nd coin a gold
    $= \left(\dfrac{p}{p+q}\right)\left(\dfrac{q}{p+q-1}\right)$

    The correct answer is option E.

    You could have solved this question by picking some values for p and q. Say $p = 2$ and $q = 4$; after solving, plug in the values of p and q in the options, and cross check which option matches the derived value. The derived value is 4/15 and matches with option E.

9. A number is divisible by 2, if it is an even number.

Between 100 and 400, there are 400 – 100 + 1 = 301 numbers. Out of these, 151 numbers are Even and 150 numbers are Odd.

So, the probability of winning a gift = $\dfrac{\text{Number of even numbered coupons}}{\text{Total number of coupons}}$

= 151/301

The correct answer is option C.

10. Probability of choosing any paired husband from group A = 5/50 = 1/10;

The chosen husband will have only one married woman in group B as his wife. So, the probability of choosing paired wife = 1/40;

So, the probability of choosing a paired husband-wife = (1/10) × (1/40) = 1/400;

The correct answer is option A.

The answer (5/50) × (5/40) = 1/80 is wrong because choosing any husband from group 1 and any wife from group 2 will not necessarily make the correct husband-wife pair.

11. Probability of getting 1st ball being green = 10/30 = 1/3;

Since the ball drawn is replaced, the total number of balls would remain 30, the probability of getting 2nd ball as green = 10/30 = 1/3;

So, the probability of getting both the balls being green = (1/3) × (1/3) = 1/9.

The correct answer is option B.

12. Say number of green balls are x, so the total number of balls = (4 + x);

Number of ways both the ball drawn will be black = C_2^4;

Total number of ways 2 balls can be drawn = C_2^{4+x};

Hence, the probability of getting both the balls being black =

$$\dfrac{C_2^4}{C_2^{(4+x)}} = \dfrac{4.3/1.2}{(4+x).(3+x)/1.2} = \dfrac{1}{6} \text{ (given)};$$

This reduces to $\dfrac{4.3}{(4+x).(3+x)} = \dfrac{1}{6}$;

We do not recommend you to solve the quadratic equation to get the value of x, you must plug in the values of x from the options and check if right hand side and left hand side are equal. If yes, the option is the correct answer.

Trying with $x = 5$ will satisfy the equation as $\dfrac{4.3}{9.8} = \dfrac{1}{6} \Rightarrow \dfrac{1}{6} = \dfrac{1}{6}$.

The correct answer is option C.

13. As per the given information , 16 questions would be correct. For the remaining 25 questions, we will have to calculate the probability of getting them correct.

Probability of getting the 10 set of question with 2 unsure options = 1/2, so we can expect that the candidate will mark $10 \times 1/2 = 5$ questions correct.

Similarly, probability of getting the 6 set of question with 3 unsure options = 1/3, so we can expect that the candidate will mark $6 \times 1/3 = 2$ questions correct.

Similarly, probability of getting the 4 set of question with 4 unsure options = 1/4, so we can expect that the candidate will mark $4 \times 1/4 = 1$ question correct.

Similarly, probability of getting the 5 set of question with 5 unsure options = 1/5, so we can expect that the candidate will mark $5 \times 1/5 = 1$ question correct.

So, the number of questions can be marked correctly = $16 + 5 + 2 + 1 + 1 = 25$.

The correct answer is option B.

14. The better approach would be to find out the probability of getting both the non-defective spanners, and then deduct the probability from '1' to get the answer. It will make sure that either one or both the spanners are defective.

So, the probability of getting both the non-defective spanners
$= \dfrac{C_2^7}{C_2^{10}} = \dfrac{7.6/1.2}{10.9/1.2} = \dfrac{7}{15}$

Hence, the probability of getting at least one defective spanner = $1 - 7/15 = 8/15$

The correct answer is option D.

15. Number of students = 20; Number of boys = 15; hence, the number of girls = 5;

So, the probability of getting 1 boy and 2 girls = $\dfrac{C_1^{15}.C_2^5}{C_3^{20}} = \dfrac{(15/1).(5.4/1.2)}{20.19.18/1.2.3} = \dfrac{5}{38}.$

The correct answer is option A.

16. The meaning of 'all the 100 shots do not miss the target' is that at least one or all the 100 shots hit the target. It would be very time-consuming to calculate the answer if we follow the traditional approach as this involves handling of 100 terms. Let us do it in another way.

Let all the 100 shots miss and then we would deduct the derived value from '1' to get the answer.

Given that:

Probability that a shot hits the target = 1/100

Thus, probability that a shot misses the target = $1 - 1/100 = 99/100$

Probability that all the 100 shots miss the target $= \left(\dfrac{99}{100}\right)^{100}$

We need to determine the probability that ALL shots do not miss.

Required probability = 1 − P(All shots miss the target)

$= 1 - \left(\dfrac{99}{100}\right)^{100}$

$= \dfrac{(100^{100} - 99^{100})}{100^{100}}$

The correct answer is option E.

17. No. of people = 12, No. of Japanese = 3, No. of Australian = 4, & No. of Chinese = 5.

We must group Australians and Chinese to make one group of 9 people.

Probability of choosing 2 Japanese out of 4 people
= Probability (Japanese = 2, Australian + Chinese = 2)

$$\Rightarrow P\,(J = 2, A + C = 2) = \frac{C_2^3 . C_2^9}{C_4^{12}} = \frac{(3.2/1.2).(9.8/1.2)}{\dfrac{12.11.10.9}{1.2.3.4}} = 12/55;$$

The correct answer is option B.

18. Probability of losing the bet each day = 0.4. It means that the probability of winning the bet each day = 1 − 0.4 = 0.6.

   Probability (Winning = 2 days)
   = (Number of ways of choosing any 2 winning days) × (Probability of winning on 2 days, and losing on the other day)
   = $[C_2^3].[(0.6).(0.6).(0.4)]$ = 0.432;

   The correct answer is option E.

19. Total number of arrangements possible = 4!

   If A is to the immediate left of C, we make AC (in this order) as one unit. Thus, there are now three things to arrange which can be done in 3! ways.

   Hence, required probability = $\dfrac{3!}{4!} = \dfrac{1}{4}$.

   The correct answer is option B.

20. Since we do not want balls of the same color, we need to draw one red AND one blue ball.

   We can select one red and one blue ball in C_1^{10} and C_1^{20} ways respectively.

   We can select two balls from the 30 balls in C_2^{30} ways.

   Thus, required probability = $\dfrac{C_1^{10} \times C_1^{20}}{C_2^{30}} = \dfrac{10 \times 20}{\dfrac{30 \times 29}{2}} = \dfrac{10 \times 20}{15 \times 39} = \dfrac{40}{87} = \approx 0.46$

   The correct answer is option D.

21. Probability of a missile striking a target = 0.6.
   Thus, probability of the missile missing the target = 0.4.

   Calculating 'the probability of hitting the target at least once' with the traditional approach would be time-consuming. The only possibility that is NOT desired is: when no missile hits the target, and thereby subtracting not-desired probability form '1', will give us the answer.

For three missiles, the probability that all three miss the target = $0.4 \times 0.4 \times 0.4$ = 0.064.

Thus, probability that at least one missile hits the target

= 1 − (Probability that all three missiles miss the target)
= 1 − 0.064 = 0.936.

The correct answer is option C.

22. Among integers from 1 to 100, the numbers which are odd perfect squares are 1, 9, 25, 49, and 81; i.e. there are five such numbers.

We can select two of them in C_2^5 ways.

We can select two numbers from the 100 numbers (1 to 100) in C_2^{100} ways.

Thus, required probability $= \dfrac{C_2^5}{C_2^{100}} = \dfrac{\dfrac{(5 \times 4)}{(2 \times 1)}}{\dfrac{(100 \times 99)}{(2 \times 1)}} = \dfrac{5 \times 4}{100 \times 99} = \dfrac{1}{495}.$

The correct answer is option B.

23. From numbers 1 to 50, the primes are: 2, 3, 5, 7, 11, 13, 17, 19, 23, 29, 31, 37, 41, 43, and 47; i.e. there are 15 prime numbers.

The perfect squares are: 1, 4, 9, 16, 25, 36 and 49; i.e. there are 7 perfect squares.

There is no perfect square which can also be a prime.

Thus, since we want a number which is neither a prime nor a perfect square, we have to exclude 15 + 7 = 22 numbers.

Thus, there are 50 − 22 = 28 desired numbers.

We can select 2 of these in C_2^{28} ways.

We can select 2 of the 50 numbers in C_2^{50} ways.

Thus, required probability $= \dfrac{C_2^{28}}{C_2^{50}} = \dfrac{\frac{28 \times 27}{2 \times 1}}{\frac{50 \times 49}{2 \times 1}} = \dfrac{28 \times 27}{50 \times 49} = 0.308 = \approx 0.31.$

The correct answer is option C.

24. Three balls of different colors imply one white, one red and one blue ball.

These may be selected in C_1^4, C_1^3 and C_1^3 ways respectively.

However, their drawings can be done in 3! = 6 ways.

There are a total of 4 + 3 + 3 = 10 balls.

Ways of selecting three balls successively without replacement $= C_1^{10} \times C_1^9 \times C_1^8$.

Thus, required probability $= \dfrac{6 \times C_1^4 \times C_1^3 \times C_1^3}{C_1^{10} \times C_1^9 \times C_1^8} = \dfrac{6 \times 4 \times 3 \times 3}{10 \times 9 \times 8} = \dfrac{3}{10}.$

The correct answer is option E.

25. We can select balls of the same color if the balls are either both white or both black.

Thus, the necessary condition is:

- The ball from 1st bag is white AND that from 2nd bag is also white

    OR

- The ball from 1st bag is black AND that from 2nd bag is also black

Thus, required probability $= \dfrac{C_1^3 \times C_1^4}{C_1^5 \times C_1^9} + \dfrac{C_1^2 \times C_1^5}{C_1^5 \times C_1^9} = \dfrac{3 \times 4}{5 \times 9} + \dfrac{2 \times 5}{5 \times 9} = \dfrac{12}{45} + \dfrac{10}{45} = \dfrac{22}{45}.$

The correct answer is option B.

26. A blue ball can be drawn only if a ball is drawn from the first box as the second box does not have blue balls.

Thus, the only condition is: Heads appears AND a blue ball is drawn.

Probability of a Head appearing = $\dfrac{1}{2}$.

Probability of drawing a blue ball = $\dfrac{C_1^3}{C_1^{(3+2)}} = \dfrac{C_1^3}{C_1^5} = \dfrac{3}{5}$.

Thus, required probability = $\dfrac{1}{2} \times \dfrac{3}{5} = \dfrac{3}{10} = 0.3$.

The correct answer is option C.

27. For a normal die, the probability of each number appearing is the same, equal to $\dfrac{1}{6}$.

However, here, their probabilities are different.

Let the probability of each odd number appearing = p.

Thus, the probability of each even number appearing = $2p$.

We know that sum of probabilities of all possible cases is 1.

Since there are three odd and three even numbers, we have:

$p + p + p + 2p + 2p + 2p = 1 \Rightarrow 9p = 1 \Rightarrow p = 1/9$.

Thus, probability of each odd number = $p = \dfrac{1}{9}$.

Also, probability of each even number = $2p = \dfrac{2}{9}$.

Thus, probability of getting consecutive 6s (even number) on two throws of this dice = $\dfrac{2}{9} \times \dfrac{2}{9} = \dfrac{4}{81}$.

The correct answer is option C.

28. The ball would all be of the same color if all three are yellow OR all are green.

Thus, probability = $\dfrac{C_3^5}{C_3^9} + \dfrac{C_3^4}{C_3^9} = \dfrac{\dfrac{5 \times 4 \times 3}{3!}}{\dfrac{9 \times 8 \times 7}{3!}} + \dfrac{\dfrac{4 \times 3 \times 2}{3!}}{\dfrac{9 \times 8 \times 7}{3!}} = \dfrac{10}{84} + \dfrac{4}{84} = \dfrac{14}{84} = \dfrac{1}{6}$.

Thus, probability that balls are not all of the same color = $1 - \dfrac{1}{6} = \dfrac{5}{6} = 0.83$.

Alternatively, since the balls are not all of the same color, there are only two possible cases:

(1) Two yellow AND one green

      OR

(2) Two green AND one yellow

Hence, required probability = $\dfrac{C_2^5 \times C_1^4}{C_3^9} + \dfrac{C_1^5 \times C_2^4}{C_3^9} = \dfrac{10 \times 4}{84} + \dfrac{5 \times 6}{84} = \dfrac{70}{84} = \dfrac{5}{6}$.

The correct answer is option C.

29. **Traditional approach:**

- $A = \dfrac{C_2^{12}}{C_2^{22}} = \dfrac{12.11}{22.21} \times \dfrac{1.2}{1.2} = \dfrac{2}{7}$

- $B = \dfrac{C_2^{10}}{C_2^{22}} = \dfrac{10.9}{22.21} \times \dfrac{1.2}{1.2} = \dfrac{15}{77}$

We can rewrite $A = \dfrac{2}{7} = \dfrac{22}{77}$, thus $A > B$; or options A and E are wrong.

- $C = \dfrac{C_1^{12}.C_1^{10}}{C_2^{22}} = \dfrac{12.10}{22.21} \times 2 = \dfrac{40}{77}$

So, the answer is $C > A > B$.

The correct answer is option D.

Logical deduction approach:

Since A = Probability of drawing two **red** balls from a bag containing 12 red and 10 blue balls, and B = Probability of drawing two **blue** balls from a bag containing 12 red and 10 blue balls, value of A would be greater than B as there are two more red balls compared to blue balls; so, A > B.

Again, C = Probability of drawing **one red and one blue** ball from a bag containing 12 red and 10 blue balls, value of C would be greater than A and greater than B as in case of C, there are more chances **one red and one blue**, versus **both red** and **both blue**; so, C > A > B.

30. Let us calculate A.

We know that probability of head $= \dfrac{1}{2}$.

Hence, required probability of all heads $= \left(\dfrac{1}{2} \times \dfrac{1}{2} \times \dfrac{1}{2} \right) = \dfrac{1}{8}$

Similarly, B = probability of all tails $= \left(\dfrac{1}{2} \times \dfrac{1}{2} \times \dfrac{1}{2} \right) = \dfrac{1}{8}$

So, A = B; it means that options A and b are wrong.

Let us calculate C.

C = Probability of getting two heads and one tail $= C_1^3 \times \left(\dfrac{1}{2} \times \dfrac{1}{2} \times \dfrac{1}{2} \right) = \dfrac{3}{8}$;

$C_1^3 = 3$ is the number of ways in which two heads may appear out of three tosses: [1st & 2nd]; [1st & 3rd]; [2nd & 3rd]

Thus, $C = 3A = 3B$

The correct answer is option D.

31. Since $x^2 \le 16$, we can see that from the numbers in the given set, '-2', '0', '2' and '4' satisfy:

- $(-2)^2 = 4 < 16$ (qualifies)

- $0^2 = 0 < 16$ (qualifies)

- $2^2 = 4 < 16$ (qualifies)

- $4^2 = 16$ (qualifies)

- $6^2 = 36 > 16$ (does not qualify)

Thus, there are four favorable values of x out of the five values in the set.

Hence, required probability $= \dfrac{4}{5}$.

The correct answer is option D.

32. We know that, probability of A **and** B = $P(A) \times P(B)$, provided A and B are independent

Here, the number appearing on each throw is not important.

Thus, the number on the first throw should repeat in each of the remaining two throws.

Thus, required probability

= Probability of getting any number in the 1st throw **and** probability of getting the same number in the 2nd throw **and** probability of getting the same number in the 3rd throw

$$= 1 \times \frac{1}{6} \times \frac{1}{6} = \frac{1}{36}$$

(Since there are six faces in a dice, the probability of a particular number appearing is $\frac{1}{6}$).

The correct answer is option A.

Alternate Approach 1:

When a die is thrown thrice, there are $6 \times 6 \times 6 = 216$ possibilities; out of which, we are interested in $(1,1,1), (2,2,2), (3,3,3), (4,4,4), (5,5,5)$, and $(6,6,6)$: 6 ways.

Thus, required probability $= \frac{6}{216} = \frac{1}{36}$

Alternate Approach 2:

Let us take the case of a number '1' appearing thrice:

Probability of getting '1' three times in a row $= \frac{1}{6} \times \frac{1}{6} \times \frac{1}{6} = \frac{1}{216}$

Similarly, the probabilities of getting each of '2, 3, 4, 5, & 6' three times in a row $= \frac{1}{216}$

Thus, required probability $= 6 \times \frac{1}{216} = \frac{1}{36}$

33. We know that,

Probability of A **or** B = P (A) + P (B) − P(A ∩ B)

There are three odd numbers: 1, 3, & 5 and there are three prime numbers: 2, 3, & 5.

There are two numbers which are both odd as well as prime: 3 & 5.

Thus, required probability = P (odd) + P (prime) − P (odd and prime)

$$= \frac{3}{6} + \frac{3}{6} - \frac{2}{6} = \frac{4}{6} = \frac{2}{3}.$$

The correct answer is option C.

34. There are a total of $6 \times 6 = 36$ cases when a dice is thrown twice.

Of these, there are six cases when the throws give the same number.

Thus, there are 36 − 6 = 30 cases where the numbers on the two faces are different.

Of these 30 cases, it is obvious that half the cases i.e. 15 would have the number on the first throw greater than the other and similarly 15 more for the other way round.

Thus, required probability $= \frac{15}{36} = \frac{5}{12}.$

The correct answer is option B.

35. There are five cards numbered '1' to '5'.

Thus, two cards (same card can now be used twice) which add up to eight could be (5, 3); (3, 5) or (4, 4).

Thus, required probability = Probability of getting

- 1st card = 5 and 2nd card = 3

    OR

- 1st card = 3 and 2nd card = 5

OR

- 1st card = 4 and 2nd card = 4

$$= \frac{1}{5} \times \frac{1}{5} + \frac{1}{5} \times \frac{1}{5} \times \frac{1}{5} \times \frac{1}{5} = \frac{3}{25}.$$

The correct answer is option A.

36. We know that,

Probability of an event = 1 – Probability of the event not occurring

Let us find the probability that '3' does not occur even once on throwing a dice thrice.

A traditional approach would be to solve the question by calculating the probabilities of getting '3' once, and then twice, and thereafter adding them; however it would be time-consuming.

An optimum approach would be to calculate the probability of not getting '3' even once and then deducting the compound probability from 1.

So, probability of not getting a '3' on throwing a dice once = $1 - \frac{1}{6} = \frac{5}{6}$.

Thus, probability of not getting a '3' on throwing a dice twice = $\frac{5}{6} \times \frac{5}{6} = \frac{25}{36}$.

Thus, probability of getting '3' at least once = $1 - \frac{25}{36} = \frac{11}{36}$.

The correct answer is option C.

37. We know that,

Probability of an event = $\dfrac{\text{Favorable cases}}{\text{Total cases}}$

Mean = $\dfrac{\text{Sum of all terms}}{\text{\# of terms}}$

The mean of the numbers in the set = $\dfrac{1+2+2+3+4+5+5+5+9}{9} = \dfrac{36}{9} = 4.$

The term 4 is present only once in the set which has 9 terms.

Hence, required probability = $\dfrac{1}{9}$.

The correct answer is option C.

38. The possible cases where one number from A and one from B add up to 9 are: (1, 8) and (6, 3).

Thus, there are two favorable cases.

Total number of ways of selecting one number from A and one from B = 3 × 3 = 9.

Hence, required probability = $\dfrac{2}{9}$.

The correct answer is option B.

39. The possible cases where one number from A and one from B when multiplied give 9 is: (3, 3).

Thus, there is one favorable cases.

Total number of ways of selecting one number from A and one from B = 3 × 3 = 9.

Hence, required probability = $\dfrac{1}{9}$.

The correct answer is option C.

40. We know that,

P (A) + P($\overline{\text{A}}$) = 1; where P($\overline{\text{A}}$) is the probability of the event A not happening

Probability of picking a red ball = P (Red)

$= 1 - [\text{P (Blue]} + \text{P (Green)}]$

$= 1 - \left[\dfrac{1}{4} + \dfrac{2}{3}\right] = \dfrac{1}{12} = \dfrac{2}{24}$.

Hence, number of red balls

= (Total number of balls) × P (Red)

$= 24 \times \dfrac{2}{24} = 2.$

The correct answer is option B.

41.

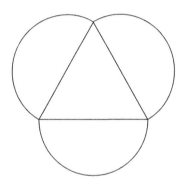

Probability of hitting the triangle = $\dfrac{\text{Area of the triangle}}{\text{Sum of area of triangle \& areas of three semi-circles}}$

Area of the equilateral triangle $= \dfrac{\sqrt{3}}{4}\text{side}^2 = \dfrac{\sqrt{3}}{4}.4^2 = 4\sqrt{3}$

Radius = half of side = 4/2 = 2 cm

Area of the three semi-circles $= 3\left(\dfrac{1}{2}.\pi r^2\right) = \dfrac{3}{2}.2^2.\pi = 6\pi$

Total area of dartboard $= 4\sqrt{3} + 6\pi$

Thus, the probability of hitting the triangular part $= \dfrac{4\sqrt{3}}{4\sqrt{3} + 6\pi}$

The correct answer is option D.

42. Say the number of green balls are x, so the total number of balls = $(5 + x)$;

Number of ways both the ball drawn will be green = C_2^x;

Total number of ways 2 balls can be drawn = C_2^{5+x};

Hence, the probability of getting both the balls being green =

$$\frac{C_2^x}{C_2^{(5+x)}} = \frac{x(x-1)/1.2}{(5+x).(4+x)/1.2} = \frac{1}{6} \text{ (given)};$$

This reduces to $\dfrac{x(x-1)}{(5+x).(4+x)} = \dfrac{1}{6}$;

We do not recommend you to solve the quadratic equation to get the value of x, you must plug in the values of x from the options and check if right hand side and left hand side are equal. If yes, the option is the correct answer.

Trying with $x = 4$ will satisfy the equation as $\dfrac{4.3}{9.8} = \dfrac{1}{6} \Rightarrow \dfrac{1}{6} = \dfrac{1}{6}$.

The correct answer is option B.

43. Probability of hitting the black parts = $\dfrac{\text{Area of the black parts}}{\text{Area of the outermost circle}}$

Area of the outermost circle = $\pi r^2 = \pi.4^2 = 16\pi$

Area of the innermost black circle (One of the black parts) = $\pi r^2 = \pi.1^2 = \pi$

Area of the 1-cm band (another black part)

= Area of outer circle with radius of 3 cm – Area of outer circle with radius of 2 cm

= $3^2.\pi - 2^2.\pi = 5\pi$

Total area of black parts = $\pi + 5\pi = 6\pi$

Thus, the probability of hitting the black parts = $\dfrac{6\pi}{16\pi} = 3/8$

The correct answer is option C.

9.2   Data Sufficiency

44. Let us first understand the question.

There are 100 coins — gold, silver or bronze. Each of them is engraved with either a consonant or a vowel.

Probability of getting a gold coin or a coin with vowel or both

= P(Gold $\cup$ Vowel) = P(Gold) + P(Vowel) − P(Gold $\cap$ Vowel)

$\Rightarrow P(G \cup V) = P(G) + P(V) - P(G \cap V) = ?$

Let us analyze each statement.

From statement 1:

The meaning of statement 1 is that P(G $\cap$ V) = 0.2.

So, the question is $P(G \cup V) = P(G) + P(V) - 0.2 = ?$

This information is insufficient to get the value of $P(G \cup V)$.

The correct answer would be among B, C and E.

From statement 2:

The meaning of statement 2 is that P(G) + P(V) = 0.4.

So, the question is $P(G \cup V) = 0.4 - P(G \cap V) = ?$

This information is also insufficient to get the value of $P(G \cup V)$.

The correct answer would be either C or E.

Thus, from both the statements together:

From statement 1, we get the value of P(G $\cap$ V) and from statement 2, we get the value of P(G) + P(V). This makes sure that $P(G \cup V) = P(G) + P(V) - P(G \cap V) = 0.4 - 0.2 = 0.2$.

The correct answer is option C.

45. This is a question on Non-mutually Exclusive events—studying French and studying Spanish.

Probability of a student studying French or Spanish or both

= P(French) + P(Spanish) – P(French ∩ Spanish)

=> P(F ∪ S) = P(F) + P(S) – P(F ∩ S)

The question is — Is P(F ∩ S) = 0.2 ?

From statement 1:

Given: P(F) = 0.8.

This information is insufficient as we cannot get the value of P(F ∩ S).

The correct answer would be among B, C and E.

From statement 2:

Given: P(S) = 0.4.

This information is insufficient as we cannot get the value of $P(F \cap S)$.

The correct answer would be either C or E.

Thus, from both the statements together:

From statement 1, we get the value of P(F) and from statement 2, we get the value of P(S). By plugging in these values in the equation P(F ∪ S) = P(F) + P(S) – P(F ∩ S), we get, P(F ∪ S) = 0.8 + 0.4 – P(F ∩ S)

=> P(F ∩ S) = 1.2 – P(F ∪ S)

Since we do not have any information about P(F ∪ S), we cannot say that the value of P(F ∩ S) must be 0.2. It can even be more than.

The correct answer is option E.

46. In the previous question, we concluded that since we do not have any information about $P(F \cup S)$, we cannot comment on the value of $P(F \cap S)$; however we can surely deduce whether $P(F \cap S) \geq 0.2$.

Let us see how?

The maximum value of probability is always 1, hence the maximum value of $P(F \cup S) = 1$.

So, $P(F \cup S)_{max.} = 1.2 - P(F \cap S)_{min.}$

or, $1 = 1.2 - P(F \cap S)_{min.} => P(F \cap S)_{min.} = 0.2 => P(F \cap S) \geq 0.2$, at least 0.2.

The correct answer for this question is option C, as we can surely say that $P(F \cap S) \neq 0.1$ (less than 0.2).

The correct answer is option C.

47. We have find out whether $x < y + z$.

From statement 1:

Say, probabilities of drawing a black, white and green balls are $X, Y,$ & Z respectively.

As per the information in statement 1, we do not know anything about the number of black balls, hence the statement itself is not sufficient.

The correct answer would be among B, C and E.

From statement 2:

Similarly, as per the information in statement 2, we know that black balls must be 1.5 times the number of green balls, but we do not know anything about the number of white balls, hence the statement itself is not sufficient.

The correct answer would be either A or D.

Thus, from both the statements together:

Form statement 1, we know that $Z = 2Y$ and from statement 2, we know that $X = 1.5Z$. So, we arrive at $X = 1.5Z,$ & $Y = Z/2 = 0.5Z$. Now, since $X + Y + Z = 1 => 1.5Z + 0.5Z + Z = 1 => Z = 1/3$.

Since $X = 1.5Z$ and $Y = 0.5Z$; this gives $Y + Z = 1.5Z = X$. It means that the number of black balls equals the total number of white and green balls combined. The answer is "No" – a unique answer.

The correct answer is option C.

48. We have to find out the probability of selecting a heart patient who smokes out of a total 87 patients.

From statement 1:

The information given pertains to all 87 patients and not only to heart patients, hence the statement itself is not sufficient.

The correct answer would be among B, C and E.

From statement 2:

If 46 heart patients do not smoke, it means that 69 – 46 = 23 heart patients smoke.

Hence, the probability of selecting a heart patient who smokes out of 87 patients = 23/87. Statement 2 alone is sufficient.

The correct answer is option B.

49. We have to find out the value of x.

From statement 1:

Probability of picking both the spanners being defective = $\dfrac{C_2^x}{C_2^{10}} = \dfrac{2}{15}$ (given)

$$=> \frac{x.(x-1)/1.2}{10.9/1.2} = \frac{x.(x-1)}{10.9} = \frac{2}{15}$$

Though you may be satisfied at this stage assuming that upon solving the equation, there would a unique value of x, we recommend that you must be doubly sure as this is a quadratic equation and it may give you two positive integers for x. Upon simplifying, we get $x.(x-1) = 12 => x.(x-1) = 4.3 => x = 4$ (Product of 2 consecutive integers). We got the unique value of x, hence statement 1 alone is sufficient!

The correct answer would be either A or D.

From statement 2:

Similarly, probability of getting no spanner defective $= \dfrac{C_2^{10-x}}{C_2^{10}} = \dfrac{1}{3}$ (given)

$\Rightarrow \dfrac{(10-x).(9-x)/1.2}{10.9/1.2} = \dfrac{(10-x).(9-x)}{10.9} = \dfrac{1}{3}$

$\Rightarrow (10-x)(9-x) = 30$
$\Rightarrow (10-x)(9-x) = 6 \times 5$ (product of 2 consecutive integers).

It implies $10 - x = 6$ or $x = 4$.

We again got the unique value of x, hence statement 2 alone is also sufficient!

The correct answer is option D.

50. Probability of an event $= \dfrac{\text{Number of favorable events}}{\text{Number of total events}}$

Here, Number of favorable cases = both the balls being green $= C_2^{10}$

And the number of total cases = both the balls of any color $= C_2^n$; we do not know total number of balls $= n$.

From statement 1:

From the statement, we know that yellow balls $= 10 + 10 = 20$, hence $n = 10 + 10 + 20 = 40$ balls.

Hence, the probability of getting both the green balls $= \dfrac{C_2^{10}}{C_2^{40}} = \dfrac{10.9/1.2}{40.39/1.2} = \dfrac{3}{52}$; hence, statement 1 alone is sufficient!

The correct answer would be either A or D.

From statement 2:

Since the probability of drawing a yellow ball is double the probability of drawing a black ball, it means that number of yellow balls are twice the number of black balls, so the number of yellow balls $= 2 \times 10 = 20$ balls.

This gives total number of balls $n = 10 + 10 + 20 = 40$. As in statement 1, we can get the probability of getting both the green balls $= \dfrac{3}{52}$; hence, statement 2 alone is also sufficient!

The correct answer is option D.

Logical deduction approach:

The question can be solved if we have the value of number of yellow balls. There is no need to calculate the value of probability; in DS, we need to be sure that the statement(s) can render a unique answer.

From statement 1, we can get the value of yellow balls equals to 20, so statement 1 itself is sufficient. Similarly, from statement 2, since the probability of drawing a yellow ball is double the probability of drawing a black ball, it means that number of yellow balls are twice the number of black balls, so the number of yellow balls = 2 × 10 = 20 balls.

So each statement alone is sufficient.

51. Say there are balls of A, B, C, and D colors. Say, if A colored balls are the most, and D colored balls are the least in number, then the question is: Is P(A) = 4 × P(D)?

From statement 1:

The least possible number of balls is 1, so D = 1, and remaining 10 − 1 = 9 balls are to be distributed among three colors—A, B, and C. Since the statement states that no two color balls are equal in number, only possible distribution is: A = 4, B = 3, C = 2, and D = 1.

Since $n(A) = 4 \times n(D)$, it means that P(A) = 4 × P(D). Statement 1 alone is sufficient!

Note: If the minimum number of balls for a color is 2, we cannot distribute the remaining 8 balls among three colors assigning different number of balls for each color.

The correct answer would be either A and D.

From statement 2:

The meaning of statement 2 is that P(A) ≠ P(B) ≠ P(C) ≠ P(D), which means that $n(A) \neq n(B) \neq n(C) \neq n(D)$. This condition reduces to the condition in the statement to 1, so A = 4, B = 3, C = 2, and D = 1. Since $n(A) = 4 \times n$ (D), it means that P(A) = $4 \times n$ P(D). So, statement 2 alone is also sufficient!

The correct answer is option D.

52. The problem will not be solved in one condition only when none among John, Peter, and Harry is able to solve. Even if one of them could crack it, the problem will be solved as they have to collectively solve it.

So, probability of not solving the problem

= P(John could not solve) × P(Peter could not solve) × P(Harry could not solve)

= 1 – P(All three can solve) – P(Any two of them can solve) – P(Any one can solve)

From statement 1:

Sum of probabilities that any two of them can solve and the other cannot solve = 1/2 means that P(Any two of them can solve) = 1/2. This is insufficient as we do not know the values of P(All three can solve), and P(Any one of them can solve).

The correct answer would be among B, C and E.

From statement 2:

Similarly, the sum of probabilities that any one of them can solve and the other two cannot solve = 1/3 means that P(Any one of them can solve) = 1/3. This is insufficient as we do not know the values of P(All three can solve), and P(Any two of them can solve).

The correct answer would be either C or E.

Thus, from both the statements together:

Even combing both the statements cannot get the answer as we do not know the values of P(All three can solve).

The correct answer is option E.

53. Probability of not losing any match = P(Both wins) + P(1 win, & 1 Draw) + P(Both draws).

From statement 1:

Since P(loss) = 1/3, thus, P(not losing) = 1 - 1/3 = 2/3. Hence, probability of not losing any match = (2/3) × (2/3) = 4/9.

The correct answer would be either A or D.

From statement 2:

Statement 2 is insufficient as we only know the value of P(Win) + P(Loss) = 2/3; though we can get the value of P(Draw) = 1 - [P(Win) + P(Loss)] = 1 - 2/3 = 1/3, it will not help us get the desired value.

The correct answer is option A.

54. The meaning of losing **at the most one** match is that the team cannot lose both the matches; it may lose none or only one match.

The probability of losing at the most one match
= 1 - P(Both loss) = 1 - P(L1) × P(L2) = 1 - (1/3 × 1/3) = 8/9.
Statement 1 is sufficient.

But statement 2 is insufficient as we only know the value of P(Win) + P(Loss) = 2/3; although we can get the value of P(Draw), it is of no use.

The correct answer is option A.

55. From statement 1:

Since both x and y are positive integers, the possible sets of x and y would be {1,4}, {2,3}, {3,2}, {4,1}. So in any case, $x \geq 1$, hence $P(x \geq 1) = 1$. So, statement 1 is sufficient.

The correct answer would be either A or D.

From statement 2:

Since statement 2 states that either of x or y is a positive integer less than 5, the possible values of one of the variables would be one among {1, 2, 3, 4}. This results in the value of the other variable as one among {4, 3, 2, 1} as $x + y = 5$.

So, as in statement 1, in any case, $x \geq 1$, hence $P(x \geq 1) = 1$. So, statement 2 is also sufficient.

The correct answer is option D.

56. From statement 1:

Since P(# of children = none) + P(# of children = 1) + P(# of children = 2) + P(# of children = 3) = 1, it means that 3/10 + 1/4 + P(# of children = 3) = 1.

This gives P(# of children = 3) = 1 – 3/10 – 1/4 = 9/20. So, statement 1 is sufficient.

The correct answer would be either A or D.

From statement 1:

P(# of children = none) : P(# of children = 3) = 1/3 will not help as we do not know that value of P(# of children = none). So, statement 2 is insufficient.

The correct answer is option A.

57. From statement 1:

From statement 1, we know that $n = 73k$, and numbers divisible by '2' are $36k$; where k is a positive integer.

If $k = 1$, then $n = 73$ and then we will have 24 numbers divisible by '3' from 1 through 73; so, the probability of selecting a number divisible by 3 equals 24/73.

Similarly, if $k = 2$, then $n = 146$ and then we will have 48 numbers divisible by '3' from 1 through 146; so, the probability of selecting a number divisible by '3' equals 48/146 = 24/73.

But at $k = 3$, we will have 73 numbers divisible by '3' from 1 through 219, but the probability of selecting a number divisible by 3 equals 73/219 $\neq$ 24/73. No unique answer! So, statement 1 is insufficient.

The correct answer would be among B, C and E.

From statement 2:

$n < 200$ is clearly insufficient since n can be any value from 1 through 199.

The correct answer would be either A or D.

Thus, from both the statements together:

Combining both the statements will give a unique answer; as $n < 200$, hence $n = 73$ or 146. In either case, the probability that a number randomly selected from the set is divisible by '3' is $24/73$.

The correct answer is option C.

58. From statement 1:

From statement 1, we do not know anything about green balls, so, statement 1 is insufficient.

The correct answer would be among B, C and E.

From statement 2:

Similarly, from statement 2 we do not know anything about red balls, so, statement 2 is insufficient.

The correct answer would be either A or D.

Thus, from both the statements together:

Combining both the statements will give a unique answer. We can rewrite $n : p = 47 : 37 = (47 \times 4) : (37 \times 4) = 188 : 148$, combing it with statement 2 gives $n : p : k = 188 : 148 : 67$.

So P(Green ball) $= k / (n + p + k) = 67 / (188 + 148 + 67) = 67/403$.

The correct answer is option C.

Logical deduction approach:

Since the probability is always expressed in terms of ratio, so there is no need to know the absolute value of number of balls, mere ratio value is sufficient. From statement 1, we get the ratio of red balls to yellow balls and from statement 2, we get the ratio of yellow balls to green balls, so we can get the ratio of number of balls, which is sufficient to calculate the probability; it means that there is no need to even calculate the value, only logical deduction is sufficient.

59. From statement 1:

From statement 1, we do not know anything about green balls, so, statement 1 is insufficient.

The correct answer would be among B, C and E.

From statement 2:

Similarly, from statement 2 we do not know anything about how many balls of each color are there in the urn, so, statement 2 is insufficient.

The correct answer would be either A or D.

Thus, from both the statements together:

From statement 1, we know that the ratio of number of red balls to number of yellow balls to number of green balls is $n : p : k = 2 : 3 : k$.

From statement 2, we know total number of balls, but not the distribution of balls.

Say, the common factor for the ratio $2 : 3 : k$ is n.

=> The the total number of balls = $(2 + 3 + k)n = 43$ => $(5 + k)n = 43$.

Since n is a positive integer, and 43 is a prime number, 43 would not be divisible by a number other than '1', thus $n = 1$.

=> $5 + k = 43$ => $k = 38$

So P(Green ball) = $k/(n + p + k) = 38/(2 + 3 + 38) = 38/43$.

The correct answer is option C.

60. Since it is given that the airplane can fly with one engine, thus to ensure that it does not fly, both the engines must fail!

So, probability that the airplane cannot fly at all
= P(Left engine will NOT work) × P(Right engine will NOT work)

From statement 1:

From statement 1, we know that the probability that the left engine will work is 4/7, thus the probability that the left engine will NOT work would be $1 - \dfrac{4}{7} = \dfrac{3}{7}$. But, we do not know the probability that the right engine will NOT work to arrive at a unique answer. So, statement 1 is insufficient.

The correct answer would be B, C and E.

From statement 2:

Similarly, from statement 2, we know that the probability that the right engine will work is 4/7 thus the probability that the right engine will NOT work would be $1 - \dfrac{4}{7} = \dfrac{3}{7}$. But, we do not know the probability that the left engine will NOT work to arrive at a unique answer. So, statement 2 is insufficient.

The correct answer would be either A or D.

Thus, from both the statements together:

=> P(Airplane will Not fly)

= P(Left engine will NOT work) × P(Right engine will NOT work)

$$=> \dfrac{3}{7} \times \dfrac{3}{7} = \dfrac{9}{49}.$$

The correct answer is option C.

61. From statement 1:

From statement 1, we do not know how many numbers have been selected, and the information about the third number is of no use. So, the information is insufficient to answer the question.

The correct answer would be among B, C and E.

From statement 2:

From statement 2, we understand that the child has to select five numbers from numbers 1 to 15.

The probability of selecting any five numbers from the set of 15 distinct numbers would always be the same, irrespective of which five numbers are selected.

For the first choice, he should pick the smallest of the five numbers.
So, probability is 1/5.

For the second choice, he should now pick the smallest of the remaining four numbers.
So, probability is 1/4.

For the third, he should pick the smallest of the remaining three numbers.
So, probability is 1/3.

For the fourth, he should pick the smaller of the remaining two numbers.
So, probability is 1/2.

For the fifth choice, there is exactly one number left.
So, probability is 1/1.

The probability of selecting five numbers in an ascending order
$$= \frac{1}{5} \times \frac{1}{4} \times \frac{1}{3} \times \frac{1}{2} \times \frac{1}{1} = \frac{1}{120}.$$

Thus, in order to arrive at the answer, we only need to know the value of 'n'. Hence, statement 2 alone is sufficient.

The correct answer is option B.

Alternatively, total numbers of arrangements out of 5, taking all at a time = 5! = 120. Out of 120 ways, only one way would have the selection of numbers 1, 2, 3, ... 15 in ascending order. Thus, the probability of selecting five numbers in an ascending order $= \frac{1}{120}$.

62. Say, the probability of getting one 'Head' on a single toss = x,

=> the probability of getting one 'Tail' on a single toss = $1 - x$

Thus, we want the value of $\dfrac{x}{1 - x}$

From statement 1:

The probability of getting at least one 'Head' on two tosses = 1 - both Tails = $\dfrac{5}{9}$

=> $1 - (1 - x) \times (1 - x) = \dfrac{5}{9}$

$$\Rightarrow (1 - x)^2 = \frac{4}{9}$$

$$\Rightarrow 1 - x = \frac{2}{3}$$

$$\Rightarrow x = \frac{1}{3}$$

$$\Rightarrow \frac{x}{1 - x} = \frac{1}{2} \text{ - Unique value!}$$

The correct answer would be either A or D.

From statement 2:

The probability of getting at least one 'Tail' on two tosses = 1 - both Heads = $\frac{8}{9}$

$$\Rightarrow 1 - x \times x = \frac{8}{9}$$

$$\Rightarrow 1 - x^2 = \frac{8}{9}$$

$$\Rightarrow x^2 = \frac{1}{9}$$

$$\Rightarrow x = \frac{1}{3}$$

$$\Rightarrow \frac{x}{1 - x} = \frac{1}{2} \text{ - Unique value!}$$

Hence, statement 2 alone is also sufficient.

The correct answer is option D.

63. The question basically asks whether the number of black balls is two or four.

From statement 1:

The statement implies that

1/2 ≥ Probability (green ball) ≥ 2/5

Say there are n number of black balls.

Thus, Probability (green ball) or $P(G) = \dfrac{4}{2+4+n} = \dfrac{4}{6+n}$

$\Rightarrow 1/2 \geq P(G) \geq 2/5$

$\Rightarrow 1/2 \geq \dfrac{4}{6+n} \geq 2/5$

$\Rightarrow 1/2 \geq \dfrac{4}{6+n} \Rightarrow 6+n \geq 8 \Rightarrow n \geq 2.$

Also $\dfrac{4}{6+n} \geq 2/5 \Rightarrow 10 \geq 6+n \Rightarrow 4 \geq n.$

$\Rightarrow n = 2, 3$ or 4. If $n = 2$ or 4, the answer is Yes, else No.

So, the information is not sufficient to answer the question.

The correct answer would be among B, C and E.

From statement 2:

The statement implies that

$1/2 \geq$ Probability (black ball) $\geq 2/5$

Probability (black ball) or $P(B) = \dfrac{n}{2+4+n} = \dfrac{n}{6+n}$

$\Rightarrow 1/2 \geq P(B) \geq 2/5$

$\Rightarrow 1/2 \geq \dfrac{n}{6+n} \geq 2/5$

$\Rightarrow 1/2 \geq \dfrac{n}{6+n} \Rightarrow 6+n \geq 2n \Rightarrow 6 \geq n.$

Also, $\dfrac{n}{6+n} \geq 2/5 \Rightarrow 5n \geq 12+2n \Rightarrow n \geq 4.$

$\Rightarrow n = 4, 5$ or 6. If $n = 4$, the answer is Yes, else No.

So, the information is not sufficient to answer the question.

The correct answer would be either A or D.

Thus, from both the statements together:

Combining both the statement, we get a unique answer. $n = 4$, thus the answer is Yes.

The correct answer is option C.

64. From statement 1:

Since there are three color balls and the statement does not provide information regarding their numbers, statement 1 is insufficient.

The correct answer would be among B, C and E.

From statement 2:

As with statement 1, statement 2 is insufficient.

The correct answer would be either A or D.

Thus, from both the statements together:

Say, the number red, green and black balls are $n, p, \& k$, respectively, thus,

From statement 1:

$$\frac{\dfrac{C_2^n}{C_2^{n+p+k}}}{\dfrac{C_1^p.C_1^k}{C_2^{n+p+k}}} = \frac{1}{12}$$

$$=> \frac{C_2^n}{C_1^p.C_1^k} = \frac{1}{12}$$

$$=> \frac{n.(n-1)}{2.p.k} = \frac{1}{12}$$

$$=> n.(n-1) = \frac{pk}{6}$$

$$=> \frac{6.n.(n-1)}{p} = k$$

Similarly, from statement 2, we have:

$$p.(p-1) = \frac{3nk}{4}$$

$$=> \frac{4.p.(p-1)}{n} = k$$

Comparing both, we get

$$\frac{6.n.(n-1)}{p} = \frac{4.p.(p-1)}{n}$$

$$=> \frac{3}{2} = \frac{p^2(p-1)}{n^2(n-1)}$$

Though we cannot get the values of n & p, we can analyze them. We see that LHS, $\left(\frac{3}{2}\right)$ > 1, thus RHS must also be greater than 1. Since all the terms of p are in the numerator and all the terms of n are in the denominator, this implies that $p > n$, and thus we can conclude that n, the number of red balls are NOT most in numbers.

The correct answer is option C.

Above approach is too lengthy and complicated. We can get the answer by logical deduction approach too.

Logical deduction approach:

We see that the scenario for each statement is the same except that instead of **Red balls** in statement 1, **Green balls** are drawn in statement 2.

Let us see statement 1.

The ratio of drawing two red balls to the probability of drawing a green ball and a black ball is $\frac{1}{12}$.

Let us derive statement 2 from statement 1. It is...

The ratio of drawing two ~~red~~ green balls to the probability of drawing a ~~green~~ red ball and a black ball is $\frac{1}{\cancel{12}}\frac{3}{8}$.

Since $\frac{3}{8} > \frac{1}{12}$, we can conclude that by changing RED balls with GREEN balls, the probability increased, this implies that number of green balls is more than number of red balls.

65. Since the team is to solve the problem, thus, even if only one of the team members solves the question, the problem is considered solved.

From statement 1:

The statement itself is an answer. The statement means that the probability that one of them can solve the problem + the probability that two of them can solve the problem + the probability that all three can solve the problem = 1/3: this is what the question asks.

So, statement 1 is sufficient to answer the question.

The correct answer would be either A or D.

From statement 2:

Given that, the probability that none can solve the problem is 2/3. This implies that the probability that at least one of them can solve the problem is $1 - 2/3 = 1/3$.

So, statement 2 is also sufficient to answer the question.

The correct answer is option D.

Chapter 10

Speak to Us

Have a Question?

Email your questions to info@manhattanreview.com. We will be happy to answer you. Your questions can be related to a concept, an application of a concept, an explanation of a question, a suggestion for an alternate approach, or anything else you wish to ask regarding the GMAT.

Please mention the page number when quoting from the book.

GMAC – Quant Resources

- *Official Guide*: It is the best resource to prepare for the GMAT. It is a complete GMAT book. It comes with a Diagnostic test, which helps you measure your capability beforehand. It features Verbal, Quantitative, and Integrated Reasoning questions types. The book contains an access code to avail GMATPrep Software, Online Question Bank and Exclusive Video.

- *GMATPrep Software*: If you buy the OG, you get a free online resource from the GMAC—the testmaker. Apart from practice questions and explanation, it also has two genuine Computer Adaptive tests; you can also buy four additional CATs and few practice questions upon the payment.

Best of luck!

Happy Learning!

Professor Dr. Joern Meissner
& The Manhattan Review Team

Manhattan Admissions

**You are a unique candidate with unique experience.
We help you to sell your story to the admissions committee.**

Manhattan Admissions is an educational consulting firm that guides academic candidates through the complex process of applying to the world's top educational programs. We work with applicants from around the world to ensure that they represent their personal advantages and strength well and get our clients admitted to the world's best business schools, graduate programs and colleges.

We will guide you through the whole admissions process:

- ✓ Personal Assessment and School Selection
- ✓ Definition of your Application Strategy
- ✓ Help in Structuring your Application Essays
- ✓ Unlimited Rounds of Improvement
- ✓ Letter of Recommendation Advice
- ✓ Interview Preparation and Mock Sessions
- ✓ Scholarship Consulting

To schedule a free 30-minute consulting and candidacy evaluation session or read more about our services, please visit or call:

 www.manhattanadmissions.com   +1.212.334.2500

Made in the USA
Las Vegas, NV
23 August 2021